Exciting

Foliage Plants

By

ROGER PHILLIPS
& MARTYN RIX

Research by Alison Rix
Design Jill Bryan & Debby Curry

A Pan Original

Acknowledgements

We would like to thank the following gardens and suppliers for allowing us to visit them and photograph their plants:
The Royal Horticultural Society's Gardens, Wisley & Rosemoor; The Royal Botanic Gardens, Kew; Levens Hall, Cumbria; Barnsley House, Glos; Gravetye Manor, Sussex; Marwood Hill, Devon; Tatton Park, Cheshire; Hever Castle, Kent; Great Dixter, East Sussex; Powis Castle, Powys; Tapeley Park, Devon; Wilton House, Wilts; Eccleston Square Gardens, London; the Savill Gardens, Windsor; Iden Croft Herbs, Kent; the Royal Botanic Garden, Edinburgh; Drummond Castle Gardens, Tayside; Crathes Castle, Deeside.

Among others who have helped in one way or another we would like to thank: Beth Chatto, Pamela Egremont, Geoffrey Goatcher, John d'Arcy, Ann & Roger Bowden, Marilyn Inglis & Anne Thatcher.

First published 1999 by Pan
an imprint of Macmillan Publishers Limited
25 Eccleston Place, London SW1W 9NF
and Basingstoke
Associated companies throughout the world
ISBN 0-330-37250-5
Copyright in the text and illustrations
© Roger Phillips and Martyn Rix
The right of the authors to be identified as the authors of this work has been asserted by them in accordance with the Copyright, Designs and Patents Act 1988.
All rights reserved.

A CIP catalogue record for this book is available from the British Library

Colour Reproduction by Aylesbury Studios Ltd.
Printed by Butler & Tanner Ltd. Frome, Somerset

Contents

Summer bedding of exotics at the Royal Horticultural Society's Garden at Rosemoor in Devon

Introduction

The plants in this book are grown mainly for their leaves rather than their flowers. They are all very valuable in gardens as foliage is longer-lasting than flowers, which by their very nature tend to fade as soon as they have been fertilized. 'A plant for year-round interest' is a hackneyed cliché often applied to evergreens, but for many of these plants it is strictly true. They may well be at their best in winter, when their leaves stand out among the bare twigs of deciduous trees and shrubs.

The woolly leaves of *Stachys byzantina*

How to use this book

Evergreen trees, shrubs or perennials are put together in the first part of the book, deciduous plants in the second; plants are also grouped by foliage colour; grey, purple or variegated foliage are put together.

Grey-leaved plants generally originate in areas with a hot, dry climate in summer; the covering of hairs or a waxy surface helps the plant to keep cool and not lose excess water. Most need dry, well-drained soil.

Purple-leaved plants are usually varieties of green-leaves plants with an extra amount of anthocyanins in their leaves. They are rather rare, though they may be a little hardier than their green-leaved counterparts.

Variegation occurs in many different ways, but most clear variegations, in which either the edge or the centre of the leaf is white, involve the loss of chlorophyll-containing cells from one or more layers of the leaf. Such variegations often produce mutants or sports; a branch may appear which is all green, or all white, or the pattern of variegation may be reversed. Some spotty variegations of otherwise green-leaved plants are caused by virus and this may be transferred to other plants of the same group by aphids.

Physocarpus 'Dart's Gold', ferns and irises in the Damp Garden at Beth Chatto's in Essex

In many plants it is the shape or size, rather than the colour of the leaf which is striking. These are often called architectural plants, and many of them are from moist and sheltered forests, and are frost-tender. Tropical bedding, in which large groups of tender plants are put out for summer display, was a great favourite of the Victorians, and is coming back into vogue today, led by Christopher Lloyd at Great Dixter, East Sussex. Most of these tender plants grow very quickly in suitable weather, and can be brought inside away from frost in winter; when put out again in summer, they will soon make a fine display. Good exotic foliage planting may be seen at Rosemoor in Devon. In California, at the Huntington Botanic Gardens north of Los Angeles, there are wonderful displays of palms, aroids and other foliage plants, as well as a fine cactus and succulent garden; there, of course, they survive outdoors all year round.

Glyceria maxima 'Variegata'

Carex

Carex hajijoensis 'Evergold' This striking variegated sedge makes good clumps of striped leaves at all times of year, but is especially valuable in winter. The broad, creamy white stripe runs down the centre of each leaf, which is around 20in (50cm) long, ⅓in (8mm) wide. It is wild in Japan, but long cultivated in Europe, and in older books this plant may be found under the name *Carex morrowii* 'Variegata', a distinct species recognized by its leaves with stripes along the margin.

PLANTING HELP Grows best in partial shade, but will also do well in deep shade without losing its colour. Very tolerant but best in heavy, leafy soil. Propagate by division of the clumps in spring. Hardy to 0°F (−18°C), US zones 7–10.

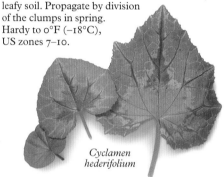

Cyclamen hederifolium

Wild Cyclamen

Cyclamen hederifolium Wild cyclamen have most attractive ivy-like leaves throughout the winter in addition to their pretty pink or white flowers in autumn. Selected varieties, such as the Bowles' Apollo group have very silvery leaves. Corms (tubers) to 12in (30cm) across when old. Leaves on the ground, to 4in (10cm) long and wide, variously marbled with silver and shades of green. Found wild in woods in S Europe and Turkey. Hardy to −10°F (−23°C), US zones 6–10. Other species with attractive winter foliage include the autumn-flowering *Cyclamen cilicium* and the spring-flowering *Cyclamen coum*.

PLANTING HELP Cyclamen grow best in leafy soil beneath deciduous trees such as oak, hornbeam and beech, or beside evergreens. The tree roots provide the necessary summer dryness. Try to buy pot-grown corms, not dried ones which have probably been dug up illegally in the wild. Plant out in late summer. Propagate by moving mature corms to a new site, leaving the seed and seedlings to come up where they fell.

Yellow Archangel

Lamium galeobdolon A spreading perennial with silvery leaves and yellow flowers in spring, found wild in woods in England and Wales and much of Europe. Several clones are commonly cultivated for their silvery leaves: **'Florentinum'** syn. 'Variegatum' is a rampant creeper with rounded silver leaves, which have a green centre and edge, and is useful for covering large areas in a short time; 'Hermann's Pride' is a less invasive plant, which has pointed silver leaves with green veins. Both are good in winter.

Lamium galeobdolon 'Florentinum'

Carex hajijoensis 'Evergold'

Pachysandra terminalis 'Variegata'

Vinca minor 'Alba Variegata'

PLANTING HELP   Lamiums grow best in partial shade in moisture-retentive soil. Propagate by division in spring. Hardy to 0°F (−18°C), US zones 7–10.

Pachysandra

***Pachysandra terminalis* 'Variegata'**   A mat-forming evergreen perennial with a rosette of finely toothed leaves, either dark green or with a white edge in 'Variegata'. The male flowers are small, with long whitish stamens; the female is even smaller, followed by white, fleshy pearl-like fruits. Both forms are good in dry shade.

PLANTING HELP   Pachysandras grow best in partial shade, but will survive full sun in wet summer climates. Tolerant, but happiest in rich, leafy soil. Propagate by division of the rhizomes in spring. Hardy to −10°F (−23°C), US zones 6–9.

Rubus

Rubus tricolor   A vigorous, creeping evergreen bramble spreading rapidly to form an extensive mat of shiny, dark green leaves, each about 2in (5cm) long, with silver backs. The stems are densely clothed with beautiful red hairs and bristles, and the white, bramble-like flowers are inconspicuous. Native of W China and introduced into cultivation in the early 20th century.

PLANTING HELP   *Rubus tricolor* grows well in partial shade in any soil. Propagate by division in spring. Hardy to 0°F (−18°C), US zones 7–10.

Rubus tricolor

Vinca

Periwinkles (*Vinca*) are herbaceous perennials from Europe and C Asia. Most have trailing stems, opposite, evergreen leaves and starry, blue flowers in spring.

Greater Periwinkle

Vinca major
An evergreen perennial forming impenetrable mats of leaves in a dry, shady position. In spring it has short upright shoots bearing mauve-blue flowers with five angular petals. In 'Variegata', the leaves have a variable creamy yellow and pale green edge. Native of Europe, and also found wild in western North America.

Vinca major
'Variegata'

Lesser Periwinkle

Vinca minor   An evergreen perennial forming mats of creeping and rooting stems to 20in (50cm) or more long, with pairs of small rounded leaves and flowers 1in (2.5cm) across in spring. Native of Europe, and also found wild in E North America, especially near the coast. There are numerous variants differing in flower colour, doubleness and leaf variegation. 'Atropurpurea' (syn. 'Purpurea Rubra') has dark plum-purple flowers; 'Azurea Flore Pleno' (syn. 'Caerulea Plena') has double sky-blue flowers; 'Argenteovariegata' (syn. 'Variegata') has silver-edged leaves and small mauve flowers about 1in (2.5cm) across produced in spring; **'Alba Variegata'** has small white flowers and variegated leaves. The variegated leaf forms such as this tend to be less vigorous.

PLANTING HELP   Periwinkles are easily grown in sun or partial shade, and are tolerant of most types of soil and summer drought provided they are not in direct sunlight. Propagate by detaching rooted pieces of runner at any season. Hardy to −10°F (−23°C), US zones 6–9.

Hedera algeriensis 'Gloire de Marengo'   *Hedera helix* 'Glomerata'

Ivy

'Atropurpurea'

'Glymii'

Ivy (*Hedera*)
is a small
genus of 11
species of
evergreen, woody
climbers which
happily creep on the
ground, forming
excellent ground-cover.
Ivies come from Europe,
Asia and North Africa, and
numerous variegated cultivars
have been developed and are grown
in gardens for their decorative effect.

PLANTING & PRUNING HELP   Ivies thrive
in shade and should never be placed in direct
sunlight or allowed to dry out. They like a rich
leafy soil and in summer can be given a balanced
liquid feed every two weeks to encourage vigorous
growth. If being grown up a wall, they should be
tied up until they become self-clinging. Ivies are
easily propagated by
cuttings taken between
June and October
when the young
growth has
hardened
sufficiently. Once
well rooted they can
be planted out or
put into bigger
pots to grow
indoors.

Hedera helix
'Pedata'

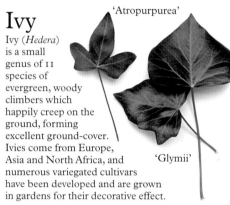

Hedera algeriensis 'Gloire de Marengo'
(often included in *Hedera canariensis*)   A vigorous
evergreen climbing shrub that grows up to 30ft
(9m) tall or more. This shrub grows well in full or
part shade and, in cooler areas will benefit from a
sheltered site on a north wall. Hardy to 10°F
(−12°C), US zones 8–10 or slightly lower.

Common Ivy, English Ivy *Hedera helix*
An evergreen shrub with glossy leaves usually less
than 6in (15cm) long. In its juvenile stage, it creeps
or climbs to 100ft (30m) tall, and when it can
climb no higher, it becomes shrubby with less
lobed leaves. It then produces greenish flowers,
which are visited by flies, bees and butterflies for
late nectar in autumn. The black fruit usually
ripens in spring. Hardy to −10°F (−23°C), US
zones 6–9. Native to most of Europe except the far
north, east to Turkey and the Caucasus, climbing
on trees, rocks and walls.
Hedera helix 'Adam'   Leaves around 1¼in
(3cm) wide, green and greyish with a creamy edge,
becoming pinkish in cold weather, and reddish
leaf stalks.
'Atropurpurea'   Leaves around 2½in (6cm)
long, deeply 3-lobed, dark green in summer,
turning purple in winter.

IVY

Hedera helix 'Buttercup'

'Buttercup'
Leaves 1½–2in
(4–5cm) wide,
suffused bright
yellow in summer and
becoming greener in
autumn and winter.
'Glomerata' Leaves
around 1½–2in
(4–5cm) wide, shallowly
lobed and very wavy.
The plant has a
compact scrambling
or trailing habit.
'Glymii' Leaves
around 2¾in (7cm
across), often unlobed,
turning purple in winter.
'Oro di Bogliasco' usually
called 'Goldheart' A very
beautiful variety with leaves
golden-yellow in the centre and
green at the edge, up to 2in
(5cm) long.
'Pedata' often called Bird's
Foot Ivy Leaves with 3 or
5 narrow, pointed lobes,
green with white veins.

Hedera helix
'Adam'

Hedera helix 'Oro di Bogliasco' ('Goldheart')

9

Agave attenuata growing along a cliff top in the mountains above Copala, Mexico

Astelia

Astelia chathamica   This is one of the most striking of all sword-leaved plants, forming large tufts of upright silvery leaves to 7ft (2m) tall in favourable situations, and 4in (10cm) wide. The flowers are green and insignificant, followed by small orange berries. Found wild in the Chatham Islands off New Zealand.

PLANTING HELP   Astelias prefer peaty, sandy soil and do best in full light, or partial shade in hot areas, with ample water and humidity in summer. Good in a large pot, brought indoors in freezing weather. Propagate by seed or division. Hardy to 20°F (–6°C), US zones 9–10.

Agave americana 'Mediopicta'

Agaves

Agaves are stiff, succulent perennials from the warmer parts of America. The Mexican spirit tequila is made from the fermented sweet juice of the flowering stem of some species of agave.

PLANTING HELP   Agaves prefer rich, sandy soil and do best in full light, or in the case of *Agave attenuata*, partial shade in hot areas, with water in summer. Both are ideal for growing in large pots in cold areas, brought undercover in winter. Propagate the offsets which appear round the parent plants. Hardy to 20°F (–6°C), US zones 9–10.

Century Plant *Agave americana*   So-called because it is supposed to flower only every 100 years, the Century Plant is a common sight in warm, dry parts of the world. It has huge rosettes of succulent, spine-tipped leaves and stems like telegraph poles, with clusters of yellow flowers on the branches. Originally a native of Mexico. 'Variegata' has white-edged leaves; **'Mediopicta'** is more striking with white-centred leaves.

Swan-neck Agave *Agave attenuata*   Very different from the Century Plant, the Swan-neck Agave has a rosette of softer leaves and a long, curving, unbranched inflorescence with masses of small greenish flowers. Wild in Mexico, where it grows along inaccessible ledges near the tops of cliffs in the pine forest.

Fascicularia bicolor

Fascicularia

Fascicularia bicolor This evergreen perennial
forms dense tufts of leaves, like pineapple tops, to
2ft (60cm) across. The small, bluish flowers are
crowded into a tight head set deeply among leaves
with small, hooked spines along the margin; the
leaves nearest the flowers become bright red in
summer. Found wild near the sea in S Chile.

PLANTING HELP Fascicularias prefer sandy
soil and do best in full light, nestling on a rocky
bank or among the roots of a tall tree. Propagate
by division of the rosettes. Hardy to 20°F (–6°C),
US zones 9–10.

Astelia chathamica

Melianthus

Melianthus major A few-stemmed upright
shrub with striking bluish leaves and blackish-
purple flowers in spring. It forms a sharp contrast
with the sword-like leaves of phormiums.
Melianthus is found wild in sandy places in South
Africa, often by rivers or streams.

PLANTING HELP *Melianthus* prefers moist,
rich, sandy soil, but will tolerate summer drought.
It is killed to the ground by hard frost, but will
spring up again in late spring if the base has not
been frozen. Frost mimics the fire it survives in the
wild, so a dressing of warm bonfire ash in spring
will help it into growth. Hardy to 10°F (–12°C),
US zones 8–10.

Melianthus major in Edington, Wiltshire

Phormium 'Dazzler'

Phormium tenax 'Variegatum'

New Zealand Flax

Phormiums are evergreen perennials with tough, leathery leaves, upright in *Phormium tenax*, arching in *Phormium cookianum*, intermediate in many of the garden varieties. In the wild in New Zealand the leaves are deep green, but cultivated forms may have pink, grey, yellow or variously striped leaves. All are very tolerant of wind and wet. The smaller varieties make a good feature in the front of a border, the larger a permanent evergreen background. Flowers are formed in summer on tall stems, and have stiff, red petals. Seed capsules are narrow and curved, twisted and pendulous in *P. cookianum*, erect and not twisted in *P. tenax*.

PLANTING HELP   Phormiums prefer moist sandy, peaty soil, but will tolerate some summer drought; they do best in full sunlight in cool areas such as Scotland and W North America, and in hot areas benefit from shade at midday. Propagate by division of the plants or by seed, but the varieties will not come true. Hardy to 10°F (−12°C), US zones 8–10.

Phormium **'Dazzler'**   A striking red-leaved hybrid with arching leaves around 3½ft (1m) long.

Phormium **'Maori Sunrise'** (syn. 'Rainbow Sunrise')   A variety of *Phormium tenax* with striped leaves in shades of pink and cream, around 4ft (1.2m) long.

Phormium **'Tricolor'**   A variety of *Phormium cookianum* with arching striped leaves around 4ft (1.2m) long.

Phormium **'Variegatum'**   A variety of *Phormium tenax* with upright green leaves edged with cream, around 7ft (2m) tall.

Phormium 'Maori Sunrise'

Phormium 'Yellow Wave'

Yucca gloriosa 'Variegata' at the Savill Garden

Phormium 'Yellow Wave'   A hybrid with arching leaves around 4ft (1.2m) long, with broad yellow central stripes.

Yucca

Yuccas are spiny herbaceous perennials or shrubs from the dry parts of North America. Their leaves usually end in sharp spines, and the flower stem consists of many hanging white flowers.

PLANTING HELP   Yuccas prefer sandy, well-drained soil and will tolerate summer drought; they do best in hot areas in full sun, and may not flower well in cool areas. Propagate by offsets or root cuttings.

Yucca glauca at Wisley

Yucca glauca   An evergreen herbaceous perennial with a rosette of grey, stiff, upright leaves to 3ft (90cm) long. The flower spike, formed in summer, can reach 7ft (2m), and has masses of waxy, downward-pointing white flowers. Found wild in dry areas in central North America. Hardy to−20°F (−29°C), US zones 5–9.

Yucca gloriosa 'Variegata'   A shrub with trunks to around 3½ft (1m), topped by a rosette to 4ft (1.2m) across of stiff, spine-pointed leaves. The flower spike, formed in summer, can reach 10ft (3m), and has masses of waxy, downward-pointing white flowers. Found wild on dunes from South Carolina to Florida. Hardy to −10°F (−23°C), US zones 6–9.

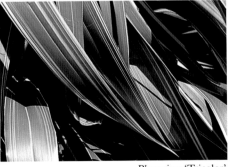

Phormium 'Tricolor'

Eucalyptus macrocarpa with *Phormium* and *Phlomis* in the King's Park Botanic Garden, Perth, WA

Eucalyptus

Eucalypts or Gum trees are the dominant trees of Australia, where over 600 species have been described. They can be recognized by their simple leathery leaves and their flowers which have a pointed cap in the bud that falls whole when the numerous stamens unfold. Some of the mountain species from Tasmania and SE Australia are good foliage plants in mild areas.

PLANTING HELP   The hardy *Eucalyptus* will normally grow in any reasonably well-drained garden soil and will tolerate drought. Their often bluish-grey evergreen leaves look good throughout the year, and are valuable as winter greenery for flower arranging. Most species grow very fast, and it is advisable to cut them back by half every

spring for the first few years, so that they resist wind better; trees left to grow unchecked are liable to be blown down. Hard pruning will also retain the round juvenile foliage of many species.

Eucalyptus coccifera   A shrub or tree to 120ft (40m) from the mountains of Tasmania, with white twigs and greyish leaves to 4in (10cm) long, 1in (2cm) wide. The bark peels in late summer, revealing smooth yellow or pinkish patches. The juvenile leaves are broader and almost round, the white flowers 3–9 in a cluster. Hardy to about 10°F (−12°C), US zones 8–10.

Eucalyptus gunnii   An upright tree to 120ft (40m), which can reach 50ft (15m) in 10 years, with spreading branches and ovate, grey-green leaves, found wild in South Australia and Tasmania. The juvenile leaves, which may be encouraged by frequent cutting back, are round and stalkless, the lanceolate mature leaves may be 4in (10cm) long, and the flowers are white, to about ½in (1.5cm) across in clusters of 4–8. Hardy to about 10°F (−12°C), US zones 8–10.

Eucalyptus macrocarpa   A usually sprawling shrub to 13ft (4m) with striking white, almost round, overlapping leaves, around 4½in (12cm) long. The flowers, which grow in the leaf axils, are large and bright red, around 4in (10cm) across. This tender gum, found wild in Western Australia, is only suitable for essentially frost-free climates. Hardy to 32°F (0°C), US zones 10–11.

Eucalyptus coccifera at Marwood Hill, Devon

Eucalyptus gunnii

Acacia dealbata var. *subalpina* at the Royal Horticultural Society's Garden at Rosemoor in Devon

Mimosa

Mimosas or Wattles, as they are usually named in their native Australia, are part of the large genus *Acacia*, containing over 900 species of trees and shrubs native to the tropical and warm temperate areas of the world.

PLANTING HELP   Mimosas will normally grow in any reasonably well-drained, preferably moist, garden soil, although they will tolerate drought. Many dislike limy soils. Though not very hardy, they can be grown outside in some northern climates, such as in London, with the protection of a south-facing wall. In cooler areas mimosas make some of the best winter-flowering trees for a tall conservatory or greenhouse.

Acacia dealbata Silver Wattle, Mimosa   A large shrub or small tree to around 33ft (10m) with white branches and silvery, finely pinnate leaves to 4in (10cm) long. Spikes of fluffy yellow, scented flowers appear in winter or early spring. Hardy to about 20°F (−6°C), US zones 9–10.

Acacia dealbata var. *subalpina*   A very compact form of the common mimosa with smaller, extra-silvery leaves, which forms a shrub or small tree to 20ft (6m); leaves around 2¾in (7cm) long. Hardy to about 20°F (−6°C), US zones 9–10.

Acacia pravissima   Probably the hardiest Australian species, which makes a bushy shrub or small tree that grows to around 25ft (8m) tall, with bright yellow flowers in spring. Its unique feature is the holly-like foliage. Native to SE Australia. Hardy to about 10°F (−12°C), US zones 8–10.

Acacia dealbata

Acacia pravissima

Camellia japonica 'Akashigata'

Magnolia delavayi at the Royal Horticultural Society's Garden at Rosemoor in Devon

Camellia

Camellia japonica 'Akashigata' usually known as **'Lady Clare'**   Whereas all varieties of *Camellia japonica* have good evergreen foliage, in some the leaves are extra-wide, glossy and healthy-looking. 'Akashigata' combines these wide leaves with a spreading and almost pendulous habit, which makes it a good foliage plant for the front of a large border, or to hang over a bank. Its flowers are good too, deep pink, semi-double and around 5in (13cm) across.

PLANTING HELP   Plant in moist, fertile, well-drained and preferably acid soil in partial shade. Best pruned in spring. Hardy to 0°F (–18°C), US zones 7–10.

Magnolia

There are around 125 species and even more garden varieties in the genus *Magnolia*, mostly deciduous trees with large, simple flowers, found in woods in Asia and North America. The evergreen species described below are two of the largest.

Magnolia delavayi   A large shrub or tree to 50ft (15m) with very large, dull, dark green, leathery leaves to 14in (35cm) long, and creamy white flowers to 8in (20cm) across. The evergreen leaves are a good backing to an exotic border. This magnolia is a native of SW China, where I have seen it growing among limestone rocks. Hardy to about 10°F (–12°C), US zones 8–10.

Bull Bay *Magnolia grandiflora*   A large shrub or tree to 100ft (30m) with shiny, dark green, leathery evergreen leaves to 10in (25cm) long, and huge creamy white flowers to 9in (23cm) across. The best forms for foliage, such as 'Ferruginea' and 'Exmouth' have leaves beautifully rusty red underneath. This magnolia is a native of SE North America. Hardy to about 10°F (–12°C), US zones 8–10.

PLANTING HELP   Plant evergreen magnolias in moist, fertile, well-drained soil in full sun or partial shade. They need a sheltered site and protection from hard frost when young.

Rhododendron bureavii

Bull Bay *Magnolia grandiflora*   *Rhododendron sinogrande* at Quince House, Devon

Rhododendrons

The majority of the 850 or so species of the genus *Rhododendron* are evergreens with leathery leaves. Many have a very beautiful indumentum (felt-like layer) beneath, and are also striking when they emerge from the overwintering bud and expand to their full size. The three examples shown here have particularly striking leaves.

PLANTING HELP   Plant rhododendrons in moist, fertile, well-drained, leafy or peaty, acid soil in partial shade. They need a sheltered woodland site; freezing wind is particularly damaging to the species with large leaves.

Rhododendron bureavii
A shrub to 10ft (3m), with leaves dark green above, thickly furry with red-brown felt beneath. Flowers pale pink in bud, opening white. A hardy species from pine forests in SW China. Hardy to about −10°F (−23°C), US zones 6–9.

Rhododendron sinogrande
A large shrub or tree to 40ft (12m). Leaves to 28in (70cm) long, 12in (30cm) wide on young plants, silvery when young. Flowers creamy white with a purple blotch, 8–12 in a truss. A magnificent species, found wild in wet forests in Burma and SW China. Hardy to about 12°F (−10°C), US zones 8–10.

Skimmia

Skimmia japonica   An evergreen shrub, native to Japan that grows to 7ft (2m) tall, but often lower and wider than tall. In spring it bears compact conical clusters of small, fragrant, creamy white flowers, each about ⅓in (1cm) wide. Individual bushes have either male or female flowers, the males being particularly strongly scented, and where male and female bushes are grown together, the latter produce bright scarlet berries about ⅓in (1cm) wide. The leathery leaves are 2–3in (5–8cm) long and have a curious oily scent when bruised.

PLANTING HELP   Plant in moist, fertile, well-drained soil in partial or full shade. Sow seed in autumn or cuttings indoors in early autumn. Hardy to 0°F (−18°C), US zones 7–10.

Skimmia japonica

Azara

Azara microphylla   A large shrub or small tree with ferny sprays of small evergreen leaves and masses of minute vanilla-scented yellow flowers in early spring. The leaves appear in two sizes on the branch, the longer around ½in (1.5cm), the smaller around ¼in (0.5cm) long. A native of Chile and S Argentina, where it grows in *Nothofagus* forest.

PLANTING HELP
Grows in any soil in shelter and some shade, with ample water in spring and summer. It may lose its leaves in a hard winter. Hardy to 20°F (−6°C), US zones 9–10.

Mahonia × media 'Winter Sun' at Wisley

Azara microphylla

Mahonia × media 'Charity'

Fatsia

Fatsia japonica   A large evergreen shrub that grows to 12ft (3.5m) tall and usually wider. In late autumn it produces branched clusters of circular white flower heads composed of many tiny flowers, each about 2½in (6cm) wide, followed by pea-sized fruits, black when ripe. The long-stalked, leathery leaves are deeply lobed, around 12in (30cm) wide. Native to S Japan and especially good in town gardens to contrast with other shade-tolerant evergreens. The form 'Variegata' has leaves broadly edged with cream.

PLANTING HELP   Any soil in shelter and shade. Water freely in spring and summer. Propagate from cuttings. Hardy to 10°F (−12°C), US zones 8–10.

Mahonia japonica

Fatsia japonica in Pimlico, London

Fatshedera

× *Fatshedera lizei* **'Variegata'**   A cross between *Fatsia* and *Hedera helix*, the common ivy. Leaves grey-green with a creamy white edge. 'Annemieke' also called 'Lemon and Lime' and 'Maculata' are also variegated. Cultivation as for *Fatsia*.

Mahonia

Mahonias are evergreen shrubs with pinnate, spiny leaves, closely related to *Berberis*. Most of the 80 or so species are found in the Himalayas and especially in China where new species are discovered every year, but there are several species native to W North America and Mexico.

PLANTING HELP   Mahonias are easy to grow and exceptionally shade-tolerant, thus making them suitable for growing in woodland under tall trees or on the north side of a wall. They prefer rich, leafy, neutral or slightly acid soil. Pruning should be done in spring, and new shoots will break from the bare wood.

Mahonia × *media*   An excellent large shrub, originally a chance seedling of *Mahonia lomariifolia* (upright with particularly stiff, spiky leaves), crossed with *Mahonia japonica* (the species with the best scent of all, but rather hidden flowers). With their bold spiny leaves and spikes around 10in (25cm) long of small yellow scented flowers, the varieties of *Mahonia* × *media* are

among the most striking hardy shrubs. The stems are upright when young, soon reaching 10ft (3m) and eventually growing very wide. Hardy to 10°F (−12°C), US zones 8–10 or a little below. **'Charity'** is one of the most popular of this group. 'Buckland' often flowers in September. **'Winter Sun'** has erect, dense flower spikes.

Mahonia japonica   A well-known evergreen shrub that grows to 5ft (1.5m) tall and wide, possibly native to China but long cultivated in Japan, and in Europe since the 19th century. The rather stiff leaves have pairs of glossy, dark green leaflets with spiny margins; the long, drooping spikes of small greenish yellow flowers are lovely to bring indoors and fill the room with the scent of Lily-of-the-valley. Hardy to 0°F (−18°C), US zones 7–10.

× *Fatshedera lizei* 'Variegata'

Box

Box *Buxus sempervirens* An evergreen shrub or small tree of dense, bushy habit that grows to 33ft (10m), and is a native of N Africa, Turkey and Europe, including SE England where it forms woods on the North Downs. Tall-growing varieties are very effective as specimens, as are those with variegated leaves (*see page 24*); 'Suffruticosa' is a slow-growing variety usually grown as a dwarf hedge.

PLANTING HELP Plant in any well-drained soil in sun or shade, although these plants appreciate good, chalky soil. Most box are easy from cuttings, though they may be slow to root and develop. Clip in autumn. Hardy to 0°F (−18°C), US zones 7–10.

Golden Privet

Ligustrum ovalifolium **'Aureum'** A shrub, usually evergreen, that grows to 16ft (4.5m) tall, often grown as a hedge, even in its native Japan. The yellowish green leaves are broadly oval, 1–3in (2.5–8cm) long. In early summer it produces clusters of small white, heavily scented flowers about ⅓in (1cm) wide, followed by the blackish fruit. A very tolerant shrub, surviving in dry shade and chalky soils. Useful for brightening up a dark corner.

PLANTING HELP Plant in autumn or early spring in any soil, in sun or shade; it may become deciduous in hard winters. Clip in late spring or autumn. Hardy to −20°F (−29°C), US zones 5–9.

Lonicera

Lonicera nitida A spreading evergreen shrub, wild in W China, with small, shiny, opposite, dark green leaves and insignificant greenish flowers in summer, sometimes followed by translucent purple berries. It makes a good hedge as it can be clipped into shape and will sprout from the old wood. There is a variety with golden leaves, **'Baggesen's Gold'**, which has the same habit as the wild type. 'Silver Beauty' has white-edged leaves and a more spreading habit.

PLANTING HELP Plant in any well-drained soil in sun or shade; tolerates chalky soil. Easy from cuttings. Clip at any season. Hardy to 0°F (−18°C), US zones 7–10.

Lonicera nitida   *Lonicera nitida* 'Baggesen's Gold'

Yew

Taxus baccata A shrub when young, eventually, after about 1000 years becoming a huge, stout tree around 80ft (24m) tall, found wild from Ireland to the W Himalayas. The needles are

Golden Privet hedge in Eccleston Square, London

A yew hedge at the Royal Horticultural Society's Garden, Wisley

Box edging and cones with purple *Verbens rigida* at Levens Hall, Cumbria

in flat sprays, the male flowers forming clouds of pollen in early spring. In autumn the fruit appears, red, sweet and sticky, surrounding a black poisonous seed. Yew is one of the most traditional hedge plants, not particularly slow growing and, if well fed and watered in summer, will gain height from 2 to 7ft (60cm to 2m) in 4 years. Other varieties are fastigiate, the so-called Irish yews, some almost prostrate, and several varieties have golden leaves. Hardy to −10°F (−23°C), US zones 6–9.

PLANTING HELP   Plant between autumn and spring in any well-drained soil in sun or shade, although yews prefer good, chalky soil. Water in dry spells until established. Be sure to buy good young bushy plants, grown in the open ground, not in pots. Clip in late summer or early autumn.

Sarcococca

Sarcococca confusa
A spreading evergreen shrub, wild in W China, with small, shiny, alternate, dark green leaves and insignificant greenish but excellently scented flowers in early spring, followed by shiny

black berries. It makes a good low hedge which can be clipped a little, or allowed to grow to its usual height of 4ft (1.2m). Another species, *Sarcococca hookeriana*, has attractive purplish stems and narrower leaves. Hardy to 10°F (−12°C), US zones 8–10.

PLANTING HELP   Plant in any well-drained soil, preferably in light shade. Clip in autumn or spring.

Sarcococca confusa

The large leaves and rampant growth of *Sasa palmata*

Bamboo

Bamboos are enormous evergreen grasses with woody hollow stems interrupted by hard nodes, found throughout the tropics and in temperate E Asia and South America. In China and Japan they are used for making roofs, for scaffolding, furniture and household goods such as chopsticks, sieves and even hats. Young shoots of many species are edible.

PLANTING & PRUNING HELP   Plant in spring in moist, rich soil in shelter and partial shade. Keep young plants moist until well established. Divide or separate rhizomes in spring. The young shoots may be eaten by slugs and squirrels. Some bamboos will spread quickly, emerging some distance from the parent plant and will need to have the new growth contained to avoid them taking over the garden; others form dense clumps. Remove any stems more than a year old in winter to leave space for the new shoots which appear in spring; this makes the clumps more elegant and less crowded, so you can see between the young healthy canes. Most species die after flowering, as has happened to the popular *Fargesia murielae* in recent years, and seedlings take some years to reach their full size.

Chimonobambusa tumidissinoda
(syn. *Quiongzhuea tumidinoda*)   A very beautiful bamboo with far-creeping rhizomes and widely branching, nodding stems 7–10ft (2–3m) tall, with narrowly acuminate leaf blades around 4in (10cm) long, ⅓in (1cm) wide. Canes of this species, with their swollen nodes, are sold for walking sticks to pilgrims on Omei-shan in W China. Hardy to 10°F (−12°C), US zones 8–10.

Fargesia nitida (syn. *Sinarundinaria nitida*)
A delicate, clump-forming bamboo, with purplish or greyish young stems to 10ft (3m) and small leaf blades around 2in (5cm)long, ¼in (0.5cm) wide. Leaves may curl in dry weather; sometimes needs extra water in summer. Found wild in N China. Hardy to 10°F (−12°C), US zones 8–10.

***Phyllostachys vivax* 'Aureocaulis'**   A tall, upright bamboo with narrow, pendulous leaves

Chimonobambusa tumidissinoda at Quince House

BAMBOOS

Fargesia nitida

Phyllostachys vivax 'Aureocaulis' at Rosemoor

and stout, bright golden-yellow stems to 10ft (3m), or in warm climates even up to 25ft (8m). Found wild in E China. For sun or light shade. Hardy to 10°F (−12°C), US zones 8–10.

Pleioblastus auricomus (syn. *Pleioblastus viridistriatus*) A creeping plant that forms wide mats of stems up to 5ft (1.5m) tall. Leaves downy, golden, striped with green, 7in (18cm) long, 1in (2.5cm) wide. Sun or partial shade. Hardy to 0°F (−18°C), US zones 7–10.

Pleioblastus linearis A tall, clump-forming bamboo with upright stems 7–10ft (2–3m) tall, with long, narrow leaf blades to 12in (30cm long), ¾in (2cm) across. Found wild in S Japan, and needing extra shade and shelter in gardens. Hardy to 10°F (−12°C), US zones 8–10.

Sasa palmata One of the largest-leaved of the hardy species, with fans of shiny green leaf blades around 15in (40cm) long, on stems around 10ft (3m) tall. Should be confined to a large tub. The related *Sasa veitchii* has slightly smaller leaf blades with white edges. Both species grow up well again after being cut down completely. Native to Japan. Hardy to 0°F (−18°C), US zones 7–10.

Pleioblastus linearis in Sussex

The dwarf bamboo *Pleioblastus auricomus*

23

E. japonicus 'Ovatus Aureus'

E. fortunei 'Emerald 'n' Gold'

Euonymus fortunei 'Silver Queen'

Variegated Box

Buxus sempervirens
'Elegantissima' One of the prettiest of the variegated forms, with narrow, white-edged leaves. Very slow-growing, reaching 3ft (90cm) high and wide after about ten years. Other less attractive variegated box varieties include 'Aureovariegata', faster-growing with almost circular leaves splashed, striped or blotched with creamy yellow; and 'Latifolia Maculata', slow-growing with large, very dark green leaves marked with yellow patches.

Variegated Box

PLANTING HELP   Although box will tolerate any well-drained soil in sun or shade, it appreciates good fertile chalky soil. Bushes may be kept shapely by careful clipping in autumn. Most box varieties are easy from cuttings, though they may be slow to root and develop. Hardy to 0°F (−18°C), US zones 7–10.

Euonymus

Variegated evergreen Spindleberries are valuable shrubs to lighten a border or a dark corner in winter. They are derived from two species from China, Korea and Japan; the shrubby *Euonymus japonicus* and

Euonymus fortunei 'Gracilis'

Euonymus fortunei which, like ivy, can be either a climber or a shrub.

PLANTING HELP   Plant in autumn or early spring in any soil, in sun or shade; in areas liable to freezing wind it will benefit from a sheltered site. No regular pruning is required other than cutting away the old damaged shoots.

Japanese Spindleberry *Euonymus japonicus*
A large, dense evergreen shrub to 16ft (4.5m) tall, a native of Japan and China. The glossy leaves are broadly oval or rounded and 1–3in (2.5–8cm) long. In early summer it produces clusters of small, pale green flowers about ⅓in (1cm) wide, followed by the fruit, a small, round, reddish capsule which splits to show the orange seed. This shrub is valuable in coastal gardens where its tolerance of salty winds makes it invaluable for hedging and shelter belts. There are several variegated forms including **'Ovatus Aureus'** a large shrub to 16ft (4.5m) tall, with leaves variously gold or gold and green, and **'Président Gauthier'** a slow-growing shrub, eventually to 5ft (1.5m), with leaves dark in the centre, shading to white round the edge, around 3in (8cm) long. Hardy to 10°F (−12°C), US zones 8–10.

Euonymus fortunei
A climbing or sprawling evergreen shrub to 5ft (1.5m) tall and wide, with round, opposite leaves at the juvenile climbing stage, longer leaves at the shrubby stage, reaching 2½in (6cm) long. As with ivy, the juvenile stage may be

Euonymus japonicus 'Président Gauthier'

Trachelospermum jasminoides 'Variegatum'

Elaeagnus × *ebbingei* 'Gilt Edge'

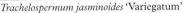

used as ground-cover. Hardy to –10°F (–23°C), US zones 6–9. **'Emerald 'n' Gold'** is usually juvenile with leaves broadly margined with yellow or reddish gold. **'Gracilis'** is usually shrubby with leaves irregularly margined with creamy yellow. **'Silver Queen'** is shrubby with large leaves, white or pinkish with only a narrow green centre.

Trachelospermum

***Trachelospermum jasminoides* 'Variegatum'** A climber to 20ft (6m) or more, with twining stems and opposite, leathery leaves, 1½–3in (4–8cm) long, in 'Variegatum' attractively marked with silver, and with pink in winter. Flowers white, scented and jasmine-like in summer.

PLANTING HELP   Plant in spring in any good soil, in cold areas against a sheltered wall. In warm, frost-free areas *Trachelospermum* will grow happily on a fence or up a tree. Hardy to 10°F (–12°C), US zones 8–10.

Elaeagnus

***Elaeagnus* × *ebbingei* 'Gilt Edge'**   Evergreen *Elaeagnus* are among the best hardy evergreen shrubs. Two species, *E. pungens* and *E. macrophylla*, both from Japan, are commonly grown, as is their

hybrid *Elaeagnus* × *ebbingei*. Very sweetly scented flowers are produced in autumn, and are followed in spring by dull reddish fruit. You will often notice the scent and find it difficult to see where it is coming from, as the small whitish flowers are hidden by the leaves. *E.* × *ebbingei* has slightly larger leaves than either parent and is tougher than *E. macrophylla*. It forms a dense shrub up to 10ft (3m) and rather wider than tall, with leaves silvery beneath, to 3in (8cm) long. **'Gilt Edge'** with creamy edged leaves is commonly cultivated, as is the yellow-centred 'Limelight'.

PLANTING HELP   These evergreen *Elaeagnus* grow in any good soil, with water in summer. They are especially useful for growing by the sea as they are very tolerant of salt. Hardy to 10°F (–12°C), US zones 8–10 or a little below.

Elaeagnus × *ebbingei*
'Gilt Edge'

Spotty Laurel

Aucuba japonica 'Variegata'   An evergreen shrub that grows to 10ft (3m) tall with spotted leaves bearing small, dark purple flowers from March to May. Male and female flowers are on different plants, so both are required for the female to bear a good set of the attractive red berries. A very useful shrub for growing in shade. A popular plant in the late 19th century, often seen in Victorian shrubberies. Native to Japan.

PLANTING HELP   Very shade- and drought-tolerant. For any well-drained soil. Hardy to 0°F (−18°C), US zones 7–10.

Choisya

Choisya ternata **'Sundance'**   A valuable bright yellow evergreen shrub to 6ft (1.8m) tall and wide. The young leaves are especially bright and become slightly greener as they mature. *Choisya ternata*, the Mexican Orange Blossom, is a rare native of Mexico. 'Sundance' was found as a sport in England in around 1985.

PLANTING HELP   Plant in spring. For any well-drained soil in full sun. Hardy to 10°F (−12°C), US zones 8–10.

Spotty laurel

Pittosporum

Pittosporum is a genus of around 200 species, mostly evergreen trees, found wild in Asia, South Africa, Australia and New Zealand. They tend to have small, scented flowers and sticky fruit.

PLANTING HELP   Plant in spring and protect from freezing wind when young. For any well-drained soil in full sun or partial shade. Can be clipped to form a hedge in late autumn or spring.

Pittosporum tenuifolium
A small evergreen tree of elegant habit that grows up to 30ft (9m) tall, with curled pale green leaves around 1–2in (2.5–5cm) long. In spring it produces clusters of small deep chocolate-purple flowers, each ⅓in (1cm) wide with a strong honey scent, especially in the evening. Native to New Zealand. Hardy to 10°F (−12°C), US zones 8–10. **'Variegatum'** is a smaller tree to 20ft (6m) with leaves edged white. 'Silver Queen' and 'Garnettii' have leaves suffused with silvery-grey. **'Irene Paterson'** is a slow-growing variety with leaves veined and marbled with white.

Pittosporum tenuifolium 'Variegatum'

Pittosporum tenuifolium 'Irene Paterson'

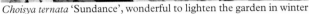

Choisya ternata 'Sundance', wonderful to lighten the garden in winter

Griselinia littoralis 'Brodick'

Pittosporum tobira 'Variegatum' A low, spreading evergreen shrub 3ft (90cm) tall, with greyish green leaves around 3in (8cm) long, edged with white. Creamy white flowers, scented like orange blossom, are formed in spring. Good by the sea and wild along the coasts of Korea, Japan and S China. Hardy to 10°F (−12°C), US zones 8–10.

Griselinia

Griselinia littoralis An evergreen shrub to 50ft (15m) tall in the wild or in mild areas, but more often only 20ft (6m) in cooler climates. In late spring it produces inconspicuous flowers in clusters 2–3in (5–8cm) long. The foliage has a unique texture and bright green colour. Not seen at its best in cold inland areas, it makes a fine shrub in coastal or city gardens where the climate is milder. Found wild in New Zealand, growing in forests. In **'Variegata'** and 'Bantry Bay' the leaves have an irregular cream margin, which is yellow when the leaves first open. Occasionally, a branch will sport to a form with the variegation reversed, called 'Dixon's Cream'; an even whiter version of this is called **'Brodick'**.

Griselinia littoralis 'Variegata'

PLANTING HELP Plant in spring. For any well-drained soil in full sun. Can be clipped to form a hedge in late autumn or spring. The young growth is easily blackened by frost. Hardy to 10°F (−12°C), US zones 8–10.

Pittosporum tobira 'Variegatum'

Ilex × altaclerensis 'Belgica Aurea'

Ilex × altaclerensis 'Lawsoniana'

Ilex aquifolium 'Ferox Argentea'

Holly

Hollies are a diverse genus of evergreen and deciduous shrubs, usually grown for their attractive red berries; most garden varieties are evergreen with spiny leaves, although the deciduous species are spineless. Male and female flowers are usually borne on separate plants and both are needed in order to produce berries.

Ilex × altaclerensis
'Golden King'

PLANTING HELP Plant in autumn or spring in partial shade. Common Holly, *Ilex aquifolium* can be raised from seed and self-seeds quite freely, but the seedlings grow extremely slowly at first. Prune holly hedges in spring; they will tolerate quite radical pruning. Other hollies can be cut back in summer. Mulch in autumn and early spring and fertilize in spring to maximize growth. Propagation is extremely slow, but autumn cuttings will eventually root. Layering is a quicker and more reliable method of propagating small numbers, especially of the variegated hollies.

Ilex × altaclerensis The Highclere Holly is a hybrid between *Ilex aquifolium* and *Ilex perado*, named after the garden at Highclere in Berkshire, England. Hardy to 0°F (−18°C), US zones 7–10.
'Belgica Aurea' A female with flat leaves that have a dark and pale green centre and a pale yellow margin, often with a few teeth.
'Golden King' An upright shrub with oval leaves 2–4in (5–10cm) long, almost spineless, with an irregular golden edge. In spite of its name, this plant is female and produces red berries in winter.
'Lawsoniana' Leaves broadly oval, 2–4in (5–10cm) long, leathery and a dull green with an

HOLLIES

Ilex aquifolium 'Madame Briot' at the Savill Garden, Windsor

irregular yellow centre. A female, often producing a good crop of berries.

Ilex aquifolium An evergreen shrub or tree to 53ft (16m) tall, bearing stiff wavy-edged leaves usually with spines, at least on lower branches, and shiny dark green on their upper surface. Fruits ⅓ in (1cm). Common holly is found wild in W Europe, eastwards to Turkey and N Iran, in woods, hedges and on cliffs, usually on acid soils. Hardy to 0°F (−18°C), US zones 7–10, for short periods.

'Ferox Argentea' Leaves are similar to 'Ferox', a most unusual variety in which the spines extend over the upper surface of the leaf, but have a clear cream margin. It is excellent for hedging, although slower-growing than many other forms of English Holly. Being variegated, 'Ferox Argentea' also makes a distinctive specimen shrub.

'Golden Milkboy'

'Golden Milkboy' A male variety with leaves 1–3in (2.5–8cm) long, spiny, creamy yellow with an irregular green margin. One of the brightest of the hollies.

'Madame Briot' A female variety with purple stems and very spiny leaves with an irregular, deep yellow edge.

'Myrtifolia Aureomaculata' A small, slow-growing variety with purple twigs and leaves with numerous small spines and an irregular gold centre shading to green margins.

Ilex aquifolium 'Myrtifolia Aureomaculata'

29

Ajuga reptans 'Atropurpurea'

Phormium tenax 'Nanum Purpureum' at Wisley

Ajuga reptans 'Multicolor'

Ophiopogon planiscapus 'Nigrescens'

Bergenia purpurascens 'Oeschberg'

Ajuga

***Ajuga reptans* 'Atropurpurea'** A creeping evergreen perennial forming mats of reddish purple leaves and erect spikes to 6in (15cm) tall, of small, tubular, light blue flowers in spring. It grows equally well in sun or shade, although the leaves colour best in an open situation. Hardy to −20°F (−29°C), US zones 5–9. Native to most of Europe except for the far north, also N Africa and W Asia. 'Multicolor' (syn. 'Tricolor', 'Rainbow') has leaves variegated with pink and white.

PLANTING HELP   Plant in spring or early summer in heavy and leafy soil. Water in dry weather. Good plants for a shady clay bank, forming rooting runners which are easily detached and planted elsewhere.

Bergenia

Bergenia purpurascens An evergreen perennial with large flat ovate leaves to 8in (20cm) long, turning purple and red in the winter. Flowers produced in spring, reddish purple, hanging down on upright stems to 15in (40cm) tall. It grows wild on rocks and cliffs in China and the Himalayas. **'Oeschberg'** is a cultivar with leaves blackish purple in winter.

PLANTING HELP Plant in spring or early summer in leafy soil in partial shade on a north wall or other well-drained position. Water in dry weather. Hardy to −10°F (−23°C), US zones 6–9.

Dodonaea

Dodonaea angustifolia **'Purpurea'** (syn. *D. viscosa*) Hopseed Bush A dense evergreen shrub or small tree to 16ft (4.5m) tall, with lanceolate leaves around 4in (10cm) long, and inconspicuous flowers followed by clusters of winged, papery fruit. Found wild in most continents, notably in Arizona and in Australia and New Zealand.

PLANTING HELP Plant in spring or at the beginning of the rainy season. Tough and easily grown; tolerant of drought, salt wind and alkaline soil, but not of intense cold. Hardy to 20°F (−6°C), US zones 9–10.

Phormium

Phormium tenax **'Nanum Purpureum'** A short variety, with arching purple leaves to 3ft (1.2m) tall. Some of these purple varieties have been found in the wild. 'Bronze Baby' is an even smaller, very low-growing purple-leaved variety with leaves to 15in (40cm) long.

PLANTING HELP Phormiums prefer moist sandy, peaty soil, but will tolerate some summer drought; they do best in full sunlight, in cool areas such as Scotland and W North America, and in hot areas benefit from shade at mid-day. Propagate by division of the plants or by seed, but the varieties will not come true. Hardy to 10°F (−12°C), US zones 8–10.

Ophiopogon

Ophiopogon planiscapus **'Nigrescens'** (syn. 'Black Dragon') A low, tufted evergreen perennial with blackish, narrow, grass-like leaves around 8in (20cm) long, and short spikes of small pinkish bells on flattened stems in late summer. The green-leaved, wild form comes from Japan.

PLANTING HELP Plant in spring or autumn in good, fertile leafy soil. Protect from drought until established. Hardy to 10°F (−12°C), US zones 8–10.

Pittosporum

Pittosporum tenuifolium **'Purpureum'** A low-growing, rather tender variety of the common *Pittosporum* (*see page 26*), it forms a loose shrub to 7ft (2m). When young, the leaves are green but become purple when they mature, towards autumn. 'Tom Thumb' is similar in colouring, but more compact, forming a rounded shrub around 3ft (90cm) in diameter.

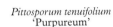

PLANTING HELP Plant in spring in good, fertile sandy soil. Protect from dry and freezing wind. Hardy to 20°F (−6°C), US zones 9–10.

Pittosporum tenuifolium 'Purpureum'

Dodonaea angustifolia 'Purpurea'

Euphorbia amygdaloides 'Purpurea'

Pulmonaria longifolia 'Ankum'

Epimedium

Barrenwort (*Epimedium*) is a genus of around 50 species, found mainly in China and Japan, where they grow in woods and on shady cliffs. In addition to this, one species is found in Europe, one in North Africa and two in N Turkey and the Caucasus. All species hybridize easily, and there is an increasing number of cultivars to chose from, using species newly introduced from China. All have attractive purplish, mottled young leaves and bloom in the spring with dainty flowers of unusual shapes. It is strange that the Chinese name for this genus is the opposite of the European, meaning oversexed billy-goat.

PLANTING HELP   Easily grown in fertile soil rich in leaf-mould, and best in the partial shade of deciduous trees. Many species are tolerant of some drought in summer.

Epimedium × rubrum   A clump-forming evergreen perennial with very attractive red foliage when young and again when old; one of the most beautiful of all foliage plants for ground-cover. Stems to 8in (20cm) tall; flowers ¾–1in (2–2.5cm) wide, pale yellow with crimson inside. Hardy to 0°F (−18°C), US zones 7–10. A hybrid between the Japanese *Epimedium grandiflorum* and the European *Epimedium alpinum*.

***Epimedium × youngianum* 'Niveum'**
A mat-forming perennial to 8in (20cm) tall, with pointed leaflets. The small white flowers, each ¾in

(2cm) wide, appear in early spring. Best in partial shade and hardy to −10°F (−23°C), US zones 6–9.

Purple Wood Spurge

***Euphorbia amygdaloides* 'Purpurea'**
A purple-leaved variety of the common wild wood spurge, which is very attractive as it unfurls in spring. A perennial with several stems around 1ft (30cm) tall. It comes true from self-sown seedlings and is shown here growing with the closely-related *Euphorbia robbiae* (*see page 36*).

PLANTING HELP   Easily grown in fertile soil rich in humus, preferring moist soil and shade in summer. Hardy to −10°F (−23°C), US zones 6–9.

Pulmonaria

Lungworts (*Pulmonaria*), so-called because the spotting of the leaves looks like the holes in the lung, are found wild throughout Europe, growing on half-shaded banks or in open woods. Their small blue, purple or red flowers are produced in the spring and the often beautifully silver-marked leaves are at their best in summer and autumn. All are hardy to −10°F (−23°C), US zones 6–9.

PLANTING HELP   Easily grown in fertile soil rich in leaf-mould, in the partial shade of deciduous trees. Propagation is easy by division in the spring, or by seed, which can produce some beautiful new varieties because the species hybridize very readily.

Epimedium × youngianum 'Niveum' at the Savill Garden, Windsor

Pulmonaria longifolia 'Ankum'

An herbaceous perennial forming clumps of narrow, silvery leaves to 20in (50cm) tall, 2in (5cm) across. It produces clusters of bright blue flowers, each about ⅓in (1cm) wide, opening from purple buds.

Pulmonaria saccharata

One of the larger species of Lungwort, with broad, often heavily spotted summer leaves to 12in (30cm) tall, 4in (10cm) across. Flowers purplish to bluish, on stems to 12in (30cm) tall.

Epimedium × rubrum

Purple-leaved Dog Violet

Viola riviniana 'Purpurea'

(often called *Viola labradorica*) A pretty, mat-forming violet with purple leaves and bluish flowers in spring. Stems to around 4in (10cm) tall. Leaves 1½in (4cm) across.

Pulmonaria saccharata seedling

PLANTING HELP   Easily grown in fertile soil rich in leaf-mould and best in partial shade. Hardy to −10°F (−23°C), US zones 6–9.

Viola riviniana 'Purpurea'

Spurge

Euphorbia is a huge genus of around 2000 species, ranging from giant cactus-like succulents to dwarf annuals. Many of the evergreen herbaceous species are valuable for their foliage, as well as the yellow-green bracts which surround the minute flowers in spring.

PLANTING HELP   The spurges shown here need full sun and prefer dry, well-drained soil. Seed is the best means of increase, although particularly good forms may be rooted from cuttings under glass in autumn.

Euphorbia characias subsp. *characias*   An evergreen perennial that grows to 5ft (1.5m) tall. In early spring each stem ends in a large, broad cluster of green, long-lasting floral bracts, each about ¾in (2cm) wide, with dark, short-horned glands. '**Portuguese Velvet**' is a particularly hairy form collected on Cape St Vincent. In **subsp.** *wulfenii* the floral bracts are a more yellow-green, with yellow, long-horned glands. Native mainly to the eastern Mediterranean region. Hardy to 10°F (−12°C), US zones 8–10 or a little lower.

Euphorbia characias subsp. *wulfenii* at Beth Chatto's

Euphorbia myrsinites   A fleshy evergreen perennial with trailing stems to 12in (30cm) long and broad bluish leaves in a rosette in winter, and with yellow flowers in spring. Heat- and drought-tolerant. Hardy to 10°F (−12°C), US zones 8–10 or a little lower.

Geranium

The genus *Geranium* consists of around 300 species. Most are hardy perennials with attractive leaves and flowers. The two shown on this page are valuable for their long-lasting leaves as well as their spring flowers.

PLANTING HELP   Plant in autumn or spring, in good leafy soil. Propagate by division of the clumps in autumn.

Euphorbia 'Portuguese Velvet'

Geranium macrorrhizum   A creeping perennial forming mats of scented leaves, which colour in the autumn. Flowers on stalks around 18in (45cm), magenta, pink or white in late spring. Tolerant of drought in summer and of full sun or light shade. Found wild on shaded limestone cliffs from S France to Greece and the Balkans. Hardy to 0°F (−18°C), US zones 7–10.

Geranium phaeum   An herbaceous perennial that grows to 2ft (60cm) tall and forms good clumps of foliage. In late spring it forms branching

Euphorbia myrsinites

Geranium macrrorhizum

Geranium phaeum 'Samobor'

Bergenia cordifolia at Gravetye Manor

stems of rather small, flat flowers, about 1in (2.5cm) wide, in shades of black, maroon, purple, grey or white. '**Samobor**' has particularly well-marked leaves, and reddish purple flowers. Hardy to –10°F (–23°C), US zones 6–8 or lower. A most useful plant for really shady places, being quite drought-tolerant once established. Found wild in open woods throughout Europe.

Bergenia

Bergenia cordifolia A very tough perennial with large leaves, the blade 8in (20cm) by 12in (30cm) remaining green in winter. Large, loose heads of pale pink flowers ¾in (2cm) long are produced from February to March. Native to Siberia, so very tolerant of cold and heat, growing well in shady places in Mediterranean climates. The bold leaves of bergenia provide a contrast to more delicate foliage such as ferns or geraniums, and were much used by Gertrude Jekyll (who called it *Megesea*), for planting along paths and on shady walls. The flowers may be damaged by late frosts, but the plants are very hardy while dormant. Other species grow wild in China and the Himalayas, where they can cover large areas of rocky mountainside. The

evergreen, leathery leaves often turn red or purple in winter (*see page 31*).

PLANTING HELP Bergenias like shade or partial shade and are best planted in rich, moist, well-drained soil mixed with humus. It is a good idea to divide the clumps every three years or so to maintain healthy plants. Pieces of rhizome will root to form new plants. Hardy to –40°F (–40°C), US zones 3–10.

Bergenia

Yellow Adder's Tongue

Erythronium californicum at Quince House, Devon

Italian Arum or Cuckoo Pint

Arum italicum 'Marmoratum' (syn. *Arum italicum* 'Pictum') A variety of *Arum italicum* subsp. *italicum* with particularly well-marked leaves, found wild around Florence and probably elsewhere within the range of *Arum italicum* which extends from southern England to Iraq. Leaves emerging in winter, around 18in (45cm) tall. Flowers surrounded by a pale yellowish spathe. Fruits poisonous, conspicuous in autumn, bright red, on a spike to 2ft (60cm) tall.

PLANTING HELP Does well in good soil in partial shade. Propagate by seed or by separating the young tubers. Hardy to 0°F (−18°C), US zones 7–10.

Arum italicum 'Marmoratum' with *Euphorbia amygdaloides* var. *robbiae*

Erythronium

There are about 20 different species of *Erythronium* found in Europe, Japan and North America. The leaves, which are often attractively marked, appear in early spring.

PLANTING HELP Bulbs should be planted in summer or autumn in partial shade to a depth of 4in (10cm) in moist, fertile soil rich in humus. It is important to keep them slightly damp during storage if they are not planted immediately. Once they have become crowded, the clumps of plants can be divided when dormant, as the leaves go yellow, but be very careful not to damage the fleshy bulbs. Seeds of the species germinate freely. Slugs may eat the leaves.

Erythronium californicum An easily grown species from N California, with mahogany-splashed leaves 4–6in (10–15cm) and cream-yellow flowers around 2in (5cm) across. The commonly grown 'White Beauty' is a little larger, but has less well-marked leaves. Hardy to 10°F (−12°C), US zones 8–10.

Dog's Tooth Violet *Erythronium dens-canis* The variably spotted leaves are 4in (10cm) long when fully grown and are particularly well marked in some forms from Italy. The flowers are produced in early spring, and are usually pink but sometimes white or lilac, to 1¼–1½in (3–4cm) across with purple or blue markings in the centre. Native across S Europe. Easy to grow in leafy soil or thin grass in half-shade. Hardy to 0°F (−18°C), US zones 7–10.

Yellow Adder's Tongue, Trout Lily, Amber Bell *Erythronium americanum* A small bulb that grows to 6in (15cm) tall, flowering from late March to June. The mottled leaves are freely produced, but the yellow flowers which only open in the warm sun, are usually sparse. Grows well in moist sandy soil under deciduous trees. Found wild in woods throughout the eastern states of USA. Hardy to −30°F (−35°C), US zones 4–8.

Euphorbia

Mrs Robb's Bonnet *Euphorbia amygdaloides* var. *robbiae* A perennial with creeping underground rhizomes and rosettes of dark, evergreen, leathery leaves around 6in (15cm) across. The flowers in spring are hidden in lime-green bracts. A good ground-cover to go with strong-growing bulbs. Mrs Robb is said to have brought a piece of this plant back from Istanbul in her hatbox.

PLANTING HELP Easily grown in fertile soil rich in humus. Tolerant of some drought in summer. Hardy to 10°F (−12°C), US zones 8–10.

Variegated Crown Imperial

Fritillaria imperialis '**Aureomarginata**' The stems appear in late spring from a very smelly round bulb. In a good specimen they can be 2ft (60cm), well clothed with striped leaves and topped by a whorl of orange, bell-shaped flowers. Crown Imperials grow wild in rocky places in the mountains of Turkey and Iran.

PLANTING HELP Easily grown in fertile soil in a sunny but sheltered place. Keep dry and warm in summer. Hardy to 0°F (−18°C), US zones 7–10.

Trillium

Stinking Benjamin *Trillium chloropetalum* var *giganteum* A deciduous perennial with a thick rhizome with upright stems to 20in (50cm) tall, surmounted by a rosette of 3 marbled leaves and fragrant, white or purple in var. giganteum, upright, 3-petalled flowers to 4in (10cm) long in spring. The plants need shelter from strong winds, and thrive in partial shade. Native to western North America.

PLANTING HELP Easily grown in fertile soil rich in humus or leaf-mould. Tolerant of some drought in summer, and good under deciduous trees. Hardy to 10°F (−12°C), US zones 8–10.

Dog's Tooth Violet *Erythronium dens-canis*

Trillium chloropetalum var. *giganteum*

Fritillaria imperialis '**Aureomarginata**'

Podophyllum hexandrum　　*Lysichiton americanus* with kingcups at the Savill Garden, Windsor

The American May Apple *Podophyllum peltatum*

Yellow Skunk Cabbage

Lysichiton americanus　An herbaceous perennial with yellow flowers in the spring, to ¼in (0.5cm), followed by huge, smooth leaves to 4ft (1.2m) long. The flowers have an unpleasant smell. Found wild in western North America. The rarer *Lysichiton camtschatcensis* has white, sweetly scented flowers and smaller leaves.

PLANTING HELP　Plant in early spring in a very wet place, even in shallow water. The plants spread both by rhizomes and by seed, and the hybrid is likely to appear where the two species are grown together. Hardy to −10°F (−23°C), US zones 6–9.

Podophyllum

The American May Apple, *Podophyllum peltatum*　This medium-sized perennial forms wide mats of green leaves in leafy woods and white flowers hide under the leaves. The Himalayan species, *P. hexandrum*, has blotched leaves and flowers like apple blossom as the leaves emerge.

PLANTING HELP　Plant in early spring or autumn in good moist soil. Best in partial shade position, but will stand full sun if the soil is deep and moist. Easily raised from seed, but takes many years to reach flowering size. Hardy to −10°F (−23°C), US zones 6–9.

Peltiphyllum *Darmera peltata*

Rodgersia podophylla in Kent

Peltiphyllum

Darmera peltata A wide-spreading perennial from California and Oregon, still generally known as *Peltiphyllum peltatum*, with round leaves to 2ft (60cm) across, on stems to 3½ft (1m) tall. The small pink flowers, which appear in spring before the leaves, are borne in tight heads on bare stems.

PLANTING HELP Plant in early spring or autumn in good moist soil, or even in shallow water. It will stand full sun if growing by water and will then colour more brightly in autumn. Hardy to −10°F (−23°C), US zones 6–9.

Rodgersia

Around 5 species of *Rodgersia* are found in the Himalayas and eastern Asia, usually growing in damp scrub and by streams. All are fine foliage plants and have branching heads of small flowers.

PLANTING HELP Plant in early spring or autumn in good moist soil. Best in a partially shaded position, but will stand full sun if growing by water and will then colour more brightly in autumn. The plants spread by rhizomes. Late frosts will damage the emerging young leaves.

Rodgersia pinnata A rhizomatous perennial that forms small clumps of leaves to 3ft (90cm)

tall, with ribbed leaflets. Small pink flowers on branching stems up to 4ft (1.2m) tall, in summer. The emerging leaves are bronze. Found wild in W China. The form 'Superba' has bright pink flowers. Hardy to −10°F (−23°C), US zones 6–9.

Rodgersia podophylla A rhizomatous perennial that forms large clumps of leaves to 3ft (90cm) tall. The small white flowers are on branching stems up to 4ft (1.2m) tall, in summer. In autumn, the leaves may turn to bronze, purple or deep crimson. Found wild in Japan and Korea. Hardy to −10°F (−23°C), US zones 6–9.

Rodgersia pinnata

39

Lobelia 'Queen Victoria' with *Matteucia*

Gunnera

Gunnera manicata A giant perennial with leaf stalks to 8ft (2.5m) tall, forming enormous clumps of stiff, prickly leaves around 7ft (2m) across. In summer, strange cone-like green flower heads, 2–3ft (60–90cm) long and bearing minute flowers, grow from the rhizomes, and are followed by small orange berries. Wild in S Brazil. *Gunnera tinctoria* (*not illustrated*), from Chile, has smaller, more pleated leaves to 5ft (1.5m) across.

PLANTING HELP Plant in autumn or early spring, in rich moist soil in sun or partial shade, preferably by water. To protect the crowns over the winter, invert the old leaves over the rhizomes in late autumn after the first frost. Hardy to 10°F (−12°C), US zones 8–10, with some protection in cold areas.

Houttuynia

***Houttuynia cordata* 'Variegata'** (syn. 'Chameleon') An aromatic perennial with elegant heart-shaped leaves and creeping underground stems. The stems reach about 18in (45cm) tall, and in summer produce solitary white flowers 1in (2.5cm) wide, with four or more white petal-like bracts surrounding a yellow-green cone. The leaves, to 2in (5cm) long, smell a bit like Seville oranges. Found wild in Japan, China and the Himalayas, growing in damp shady hillsides, and woods. The leaves can be eaten like spinach, and are much collected in the mountains of W China and sold in local markets. They have a strong ginger-like flavour. **'Variegata'** has leaves heavily variegated with cream and crimson, and is very colourful throughout the summer.

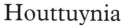

Rheum palmatum 'Atrosanguineum'

Houttuynia cordata 'Variegata'

Veratrum nigrum

Imperata cylindrica 'Rubra'

PLANTING HELP Plant in autumn or early spring, in any moist soil in sun or shade. Hardy to 0°F (–18°C), US zones 7–10.

Imperata

Imperata cylindrica **'Rubra'** An upright perennial grass with striking red leaves 8–20in (20–50cm) tall, ¼–½in (0.5–1.5cm) wide. This grass grows wild in waste places in eastern Asia, and is easily grown in ordinary garden soil. Keep well watered in summer.

PLANTING HELP Plant in autumn or spring, in any moist soil in sun or partial shade. Hardy to 10°F (–12°C), US zones 8–10.

Lobelia

Lobelia **'Queen Victoria'** This is one of the finest of a group of purple-leaved, large-flowered perennial lobelias, flowering in late summer. Stems to 3½ft (1m). Flowers bright red, around 3in (8cm) long. A hybrid between various North American and Mexican species.

PLANTING HELP Plant in spring or early summer in a moist fertile border in sun or partial shade. Cover established plants in winter with dry peat or bark. In colder areas, lift the plants and overwinter them under cover to protect them from frost, wet and slugs. Hardy to 10°F (–12°C), US zones 8–10.

Rheum

Rheum palmatum **'Atrosanguineum'** A huge plant from a very stout woody stock, with leaves up to 3ft (90cm) long, bright red and purple as they emerge from the ground. Flowers pink, in tall spikes to 10ft (3m) or more, or white in the normal, green-leaved form. Found wild in W China.

PLANTING HELP Plant in spring or early summer in a moist, fertile border in sun or partial shade, ideally close to water. All rheums require very rich, moist soil, well-manured each year, to grow and flower to their full potential. Hardy to –10°F (–23°C), US zones 6–9.

Veratrum

Veratrum nigrum A perennial with hairless pleated leaves and spikes to 4½ft (1.3m) tall of small black flowers, smelling of rotten plums. Found wild from France to China and Korea. There are around 15 species of *Veratrum*; the two most often grown are *V. viride* and *V. album*.

PLANTING HELP Plant in spring or early summer in a moist, fertile border in sun or partial shade. All Veratrums require very rich soil, well-manured each year, to grow and flower well. Propagate by division or by seed, which will take several years to make a flowering-sized plant. Hardy to –30°F (–35°C), US zones 4–10.

Gunnera manicata at Tatton Park, Cheshire

Japanese Maples

Maples have long been valued and collected by
Japanese gardeners for their elegance,
great diversity and fine autumn colour.
Over 200 named varieties are cultivated at
present. Most are particularly beautiful as
the young leaves emerge in spring. Most of
the cultivated varieties are derived from the
species *Acer palmatum*.

Acer
'Sango-kaku'

PLANTING HELP   Japanese maples do best
in moist, acid soil sheltered from the wind and in
the dappled shade of larger trees. Plant in late
autumn or early spring. Water in dry periods until
well established. Hardy to −20°F (−29°C), US
zones 5–9.

Acer palmatum   A shrub or tree to 33ft (10m),
found wild in E China, Korea and Japan. Leaves
5–7-lobed, to around 2¾in (7cm) across. Flowers
purplish, in hanging bunches, fruit often reddish.
'Elegans', a low, spreading tree to 10ft (3m) when
old, has dissected leaves with toothed leaflets,
bronze in the spring, bright orange and red in
autumn. **'Linearilobum'**, a low, spreading and
dense shrub or small tree to 13ft (4m) when old,
with green leaves dissected nearly to the base into
narrow, untoothed lobes. **'Sango-kaku'** (also
known as 'Senkaki' and Coral Bark Maple) is a
small, rather upright tree to 24ft (7m) when
mature, noted for its bright coral-red twigs. Leaves
bright golden-yellow in autumn. **'Shindeshojo'** is
a low, rounded shrub to 7ft (2m) in diameter, with
the young leaves bright pinkish-red or crimson
scarlet, remaining red into early summer, when it
then become green and pink mottled. This variety
needs particularly sheltered conditions.

**The Golden Full Moon
Maple** *Acer shirasawanum* f. *aureum*
(syn. *Acer japonicum* 'Aureum')   A small shrub or
stout flat-topped tree to 13ft (4m) tall with golden
9–13- lobed leaves and small bunches of red
flowers in spring, followed by red fruit. The
species is wild in central and S Japan; the golden
form is the one usually seen in gardens, and is
tougher than the forms of *Acer palmatum*. Autumn
colour yellow, orange, red and purple. Hardy to
−20°F (−29°C), US zones 5–10.

Photinia

Photinia × *fraseri* **'Red Robin'**   An evergreen
shrub that grows to 20ft (6m) tall and usually as
wide. The new growth, which is produced
throughout the summer, is bright red. The small
white flowers, produced in late spring in broad
clusters are each about ½in (1.5cm) wide. *Photinia*
× *fraseri* is a hybrid first raised in the USA, but
'Red Robin' originated in New Zealand.

Acer palmatum 'Linearilobum' at the Savill Garden, Windsor

Photinia × *fraseri* 'Red Robin'

PLANTING HELP   Plant in fertile, moist, well-drained soil in sun or partial shade. Unlike *Pieris*, *Photinia* grows well in limy soils. Hardy to 0°F (−18°C), US zones 7–10.

Pieris

A genus of 7 species of evergreen shrubs from North America, Japan, China and the Himalayas. They are well worth growing for their flowers alone, but in some species these are eclipsed by the intense red or yellow young foliage.

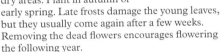

Pieris 'Forest Flame'

PLANTING HELP   *Pieris* thrive in similar conditions to rhododendrons; acid, leafy soil, with some shade in hot, dry areas. Plant in autumn or early spring. Late frosts damage the young leaves, but they usually come again after a few weeks. Removing the dead flowers encourages flowering the following year.

Pieris formosa   A vigorous evergreen shrub to 8ft (2.5m) tall, producing drooping clusters 4in (10cm) long, crowded with small, bell-shaped white flowers, each ⅓in (1cm) long, and slightly scented, in early spring. The leaves have a rough surface, and are around 1¼in (3cm) wide. The new shoots are brownish, or bright red especially in var. *forrestii*, in early spring, gradually changing through creamy pink to the dark green of summer. Hardy to 10°F (−12°C), US zones 8–10.

Pieris 'Forest Flame'   A hybrid between the Japanese *Pieris japonica* and the Chinese *Pieris formosa*, with particularly bright scarlet young shoots and narrower leaves than *Pieris forrestii*. Hardy to 0°F (−18°C), US zones 7–10.

Pieris formosa

Acer palmatum 'Shindeshojo'

Acer palmatum 'Elegans'

The Golden Full Moon Maple

Acanthus mollis var. *latifolius*

Lady's Mantle *Alchemilla mollis*

Hosta 'Royal Standard'

Hosta 'Devon Green' at Cleave House, Devon

Hosta kikutii

Acanthus

Acanthus mollis   A vigorous perennial that
forms wide clumps of shiny, dark green, deeply
divided leaves around 3ft (90cm) long. In summer
it produces erect stems to 7ft (2m) tall, with many
hooded whitish flowers, 2in (5cm) long. Found
wild mainly in the western Mediterranean, where
its leaves often emerge in autumn. **Var. *latifolius***
has broader leaves. *Acanthus spinosus* is very
similar but with deeper, cut, spiny leaves.

PLANTING HELP   Plant in autumn or early
spring in any well-drained soil in sun or partial
shade. Drought-tolerant and liable to attack by a
white mildew in humid weather. Snails and slugs
often spoil the young leaves. Hardy to 10°F
(−12°C), US zones 8–10.

Lady's Mantle

Alchemilla mollis   A perennial with softly hairy,
pale green, fan-shaped leaves up to 6in (15cm)
across, on stalks 1ft (30cm) long. In summer it
produces airy sprays of tiny yellow flowers around
18in (45cm) tall, held well above the foliage.
Found wild from Greece to the Caucasus and
N Iran. This is seen at its best after a shower when
the hairs trap glistening raindrops.

PLANTING HELP   Plant in autumn or early
spring in any soil in sun or partial shade. As it may
self-seed freely, it is often wise to cut off the flower

Solomon's Seal *Polygonatum* × *hybridum* at the Royal Horticultural Society's Garden at Wisley

heads as they start to turn brown. It is quite drought-tolerant. Hardy to −20°F (−29°C), US zones 5–10.

Hosta

Hostas are among the best foliage plants. Because they are unstable genetically, they are very diverse, and their elegant, ribbed leaves vary greatly in size and colour, occurring in yellow, blue-grey and variegated forms, as well as the normal green. The Japanese were the early fanciers and breeders of hostas, and the first garden varieties were introduced from Japan in the 19th century. Many new ones have since been raised in Europe, and even more in eastern North America, where the hot, wet summers are ideal for optimum growth. Over 1000 have now been named. Hostas associate very well with ferns and shade-loving grasses.

PLANTING HELP   Plant in autumn or early spring in deep, rich, leafy soil in partial shade, or full sun in cloudy areas. Leaf colours develop best in full light, but hot sun will scorch the leaves. Protect from slugs and snails, especially when the leaves are young. Most hostas are hardy to −40°F (−40°C), US zones 3–10, but in cold areas should be well mulched in autumn.

Hosta **'Devon Green'**   This new variety has stiff, deeply ribbed leaves, forming a mound of foliage around 2ft (60cm) across. Flowers pale mauve. A green sport of the well-known grey-leaved 'Halcyon'.

Hosta kikutii   A species with rather rounded leaf blades, with a long acuminate point, found wild in S Japan in Kyushu. Flowers white, on a tall stem with broad bracts, in late summer.

Hosta **'Royal Standard'** (syn. *Hosta* 'Wayside Perfection')   A hybrid between *Hosta plantaginea* and possibly *Hosta sieboldii*, this forms a mound to 2ft (60cm) tall and 15in (40cm) wide of heart-shaped leaves 10 × 7in (25 × 18cm), and produces an arching stem of fragrant white funnel-shaped flowers in late summer. Rapid and vigorous growth make this an excellent ground-cover or landscaping plant. Shade to three-quarters sun.

Solomon's Seal

Polygonatum × *hybridum*   A rhizomatous perennial with arching stems to 3ft (90cm) long. The alternate, oval leaves are around 5in (13cm) long, and the small greenish flowers hang down in bunches of 4. The round red berries are seldom formed in this hybrid.

PLANTING HELP   Easily grown in leafy soil in shade or partial shade in cool areas. Propagate by dividing the rhizomes in early spring or late summer. Hardy to −40°F (−40°C), US zones 3–8.

Vitis coignetiae at Hever

Amicia zygomeris in flower

Exotic plantings for summer

Though many of the plants on these pages will not survive much frost, they can still be used with great effect in temperate gardens in Europe and North America. Some, such as *Amicia* and *Canna*, are cut to the ground in winter, but with a deep mulch, will survive and grow again quickly in spring. Others such as *Cordyline* or *Ensete* will survive a few degrees of frost, and can either be brought indoors or wrapped up for the coldest months of the year.

Amicia

Amicia zygomeris   A sub-shrub to 7ft (2m) or more, with distinctive, bluish green, pinnate leaves and large, round, purplish stipules. In late summer, small yellow, purple-veined pea flowers are produced among the leaves. Found wild in W Mexico.

PLANTING HELP   Plant in spring in deep, well-drained soil, in sun. Cover with a deep, dry mulch in winter. Hardy to 32°F (0°C), US zones 10–11.

Banana

Ensete ventricosum 'Rubrum'   In tropical areas this can form a tall perennial to 40ft (12m), with a trunk and a rosette of leaves 10–20ft (3–6m) long. Young plants are of more manageable proportions, around 7ft (2m) across. The fruits are dry and inedible.

PLANTING HELP   Plant in spring in rich, moist soil, in sun or partial shade, and in as sheltered a site as possible. Feed and water well through the summer. Hardy to 32°F (0°C), US zones 10–11.

Canna musifolia at Rosemoor

Canna

Canna musifolia   A perennial with tuberous rhizomes and upright stems to 5ft (1.5m) tall. Leaves bluish with purplish markings. Flowers upright, small and red. *Canna iridiflora* is taller

Exotics at the Royal Horticultural Society's Garden at Rosemoor   *Cordyline indivisa*

and equally exotic, to 7ft (2m) or more, with hanging tubular pinkish-red flowers.

PLANTING HELP   Plant in spring in rich, moist soil, in sun or partial shade. Lift in winter, or protect from frost with a deep mulch. Hardy to 32°F (0°C), US zones 10–11.

Cordyline

Cordyline indivisa   This eventually forms a tree to 25ft (8m), with leaves to 7ft (2m) long, 6in (15cm) wide, bluish green on the underside. Wild in New Zealand in wet evergreen forests.

PLANTING HELP   Plant in spring in any good, leafy soil, in sun or partial shade. Hardy to 32°F (0°C), US zones 10–11 or in the warmer parts of zone 9.

Vitis coignetiae

Vitis coignetiae   A magnificent deciduous climber that can reach 80ft (24m) tall, given suitable support, such as a wall or a tall tree. The handsome leaves to 1ft (30cm) across, are covered with a fawn felt on the underside and turn to brilliant orange, red and purple in autumn. Found wild in the forests of N Japan and Korea.

PLANTING HELP   Plant in autumn or spring in deep, rich soil, in sun or partial shade. No pruning is required, other than to control its spread. Hardy to –10°F (–23°C), US zones 6–9.

Ensete ventricosum 'Rubrum' with a rosette of *Echium wildpretii*

47

Ferns & Mosses

Ferns and mosses are typical plants of shady, moist woods, and their soft forms and cool greens are ideal for producing a natural effect in the garden. Those shown here are only a minute sample of the many ferns available.

PLANTING HELP   Most ferns and mosses prefer moist, but not very wet, shade or partial shade. Propagate by division. Drought and drying wind are their chief enemies, and fern roots are often attacked by vine weevil grubs. Mosses will not tolerate being covered with dead leaves.

Maidenhair Fern *Adiantum pedatum*
A delicate deciduous fern from moist woods in North America and NE Asia. Stems forming clumps of fronds to 1½ft (45cm) tall, with delicate radiating segments. Hardy to −30°F (−35°C), US zones 4–8, but needs cool, humid shade.

Maidenhair Fern *Adiantum pedatum*

Matteuccia struthiopteris
The Shuttlecock Fern

Polystichum setiferum 'Lineare'

Athyrium niponicum var. *pictum*

Ferns and the moss *Polytrichum commune* in the Japanese garden at Tatton Park, Cheshire

Athyrium niponicum* var. *pictum This form of the Japanese Lady Fern is one of the few ferns with coloured fronds; they are deciduous, marked with silvery gray and purple, and are 12–20in (30–50cm) long. Hardy to –10°F (–23°C), US zones 6–9.

Leucobryum glaucum A pretty, silvery green moss which can be grown in dry shade, but needs acid soil to survive. Clumps are found detached from the ground and these form the usual method of propagation, both in nature and in the garden. Hardy to –10°F (–23°C), US zones 6–9.

Matteuccia struthiopteris The Shuttlecock Fern is a deciduous fern found wild throughout the northern hemisphere, with pale green shuttlecocks of sterile fronds 2–4ft (60–120cm) tall in early spring, and stiff, fertile fronds in summer. This fern spreads by underground runners to form large patches in damp areas. Hardy to –10°F (–23°C), US zones 6–9.

***Polystichum setiferum* 'Lineare'** A form of the wild Soft Prickly Shield Fern with very narrow leaflets. An evergreen fern with fronds to 1½ft (45cm) long, easily grown in light shade. One of the tougher ferns for the garden. *Polystichum setiferum* has given rise to many varieties, such as the 'Divisilobum' group with very soft, feathery fronds. Hardy to –10°F (–23°C), US zones 6–9.

Polytrichum commune One of the largest and toughest mosses, with wiry stems to 10in (25cm) or more in old patches, and dark green, pointed leaves. This moss is used in Japanese gardens as ground-cover under trees, and will also make a good edging, and may appear on old peat blocks. It needs acid soil. Hardy to –30°F (–35°C), US zones 4–8.

Leucobryum glaucum

Hakonechloa macra 'Aureola' with *Rodgersia* at the Savill Gardens, Windsor

Bowles' Golden Sedge

Carex elata **'Aurea'**   A clump-forming perennial to 2ft (60cm) tall, with erect or arching long, grass-like leaves, slender but stiff, bright yellow in spring, becoming greener by late summer. Hardy to −10°F (−23°C), US zones 6–9.

PLANTING HELP   Found wild in wet places in Europe, and best grown at the edge of a pond or stream. Divide the clumps in spring.

Bowles' Golden Sedge at Wilton House

Hakonechloa

Hakonechloa macra **'Aureola'**   A beautiful deciduous grass forming dense clumps of arching stems 15–27in (40–70cm) long, with flat golden-striped leaves. Found growing wild on wet cliffs in the mountains of Japan.

PLANTING HELP   Plant in spring in heavy well-drained soil in partial shade. Propagate by division in spring or summer. Hardy to 0°F (−18°C), US zones 7–10.

Hosta

Shown here are some of the golden-leaved hostas. Their colour develops best when they are grown in full light; in the shade their leaves stay green.

PLANTING HELP   Plant in autumn or early spring in deep, rich, leafy soil in partial shade, or full sun in cloudy areas. Protect from slugs and snails, especially when the leaves are young. Most hostas are hardy to −40°F (−40°C), US zones 3–10, but in cold areas should be well mulched in autumn.

Hosta **'Piedmont Gold'**   A medium-sized hosta which forms a mound to 2½ft (75cm) wide. The smooth, bright golden leaves with wavy edges are 10in (25cm) long, and 5in (13cm) wide. The funnel-shaped lavender flowers appear in midsummer. Best in half sun.

Hosta 'Piedmont Gold' at Cleave House, Devon

Hosta 'Birchwood Parky's Gold'

Hosta 'Birchwood Parky's Gold' This hosta forms a mound of golden heart-shaped leaves up to 1½ft (45cm) tall and 2½ft (75cm) wide. The bell-shaped flowers are lilac and bloom in summer. Grows in shade to three-quarters sun.

Hosta 'Daybreak' A large hosta which forms a mound to 20in (50cm) high and 3⅓ft (1m) wide. The smooth, golden-metallic leaves with wavy edges are 12in (30cm) long and 8in (20cm) wide. The funnel-shaped pale lavender flowers appear in midsummer. Best in half sun. A cultivar developed from *Hosta montana*.

Hosta 'Daybreak'

Creeping Jenny

Lysimachia nummularia **'Aurea'** A creeping perennial with stems that root as they go, pairs of small round leaves around 1in (2.5cm) across and small yellow cup-shaped flowers, each about ⅓in (1cm) wide. Can be invasive in heavy soils. Over a long period, from spring to late summer, it produces a succession of small yellow flowers. The normal green-leaved variety is found wild in Europe and western Asia.

PLANTING HELP Plant in moist fertile soil in partial shade and propagate by division in spring or autumn. Hardy to −20°F (−29°C), US zones 5–9.

Lysimachia nummularia 'Aurea' with the flowers of *Campanula portenschlagiana*

Golden Lemon Balm

Melissa officinalis **'Aurea'**   Sometimes called Bee Balm, this perennial is native to S Europe, but naturalized in Britain and parts of North America. It makes a bush up to about 2ft (60cm) tall with bright golden young leaves, becoming green then speckled later, and small whitish yellow flowers during the summer and early autumn. The leaves have a delicate lemon scent and can be dried and used as tea or in pot pourri.

PLANTING HELP   Lemon Balm grows well in almost any soil, in sun or shade. It can be invasive, as it seeds itself and spreads by means of a creeping woody rootstock, but it is nevertheless a good, tough plant for a spot at the edge of a path where it can be brushed against. Hardy to –10°F (–23°C), US zones 6–9 or less.

Golden Dead Nettle

Golden Meadow-sweet
Filipendula ulmaria 'Aurea'

Golden Meadow-sweet

Filipendula ulmaria **'Aurea'**   A perennial with bright golden-yellow leaves especially in the spring. The flowering stems grow to 5ft (1.5m) tall and produce frothy sprays of small, creamy white flowers in late summer. The normal green form is found wild in marshes and damp hedgerows throughout Europe and Asia.

PLANTING HELP   Grows in any moist or wet soil; useful as a bright accent in a meadow or bog garden. Hardy to –30°F (–35°C), US zones 4–8.

Golden Hop

Humulus lupulus **'Aureus'**   A yellow-leaved variety of the common hop, which is a twining herbaceous perennial with stems that grow to 20ft (6m) tall. The female flowers, which are found in the golden form, develop into hops in August. Native to Europe and western and central Asia.

PLANTING HELP   Grows in any soil, preferably in a warm, sheltered position. A useful plant to cover an unsightly shed or fence, drought-resistant once established. Hardy to 0°F (–18°C), US zones 7–10.

Golden Dead Nettle

Lamium maculatum **'Golden Nuggets'**
A creeping, mat-forming perennial which has golden leaves with a silver flash down the centre of each, flowering stems to 7in (18cm) and pink flowers in spring. *Lamium maculatum* 'Aureum' is very similar, but has less bright leaves.

PLANTING HELP   Grows in any soil, preferably in a cool, sheltered position, with a loose, leafy soil. Protect from slugs and snails. Hardy to 0°F (–18°C), US zones 7–10.

Primrose Heron

Stachys byzantina **'Primrose Heron'**   This golden-leaved variety of the familiar Lamb's Ears forms a mat of woolly leaves, yellow-green under the white wool. The flowering stems may reach to around 1½ft (45cm) with whorls of small, purplish pink flowers.

PLANTING HELP   'Primrose Heron' will grow well in almost any good, well-drained soil, in sun or light shade. Hardy to 0°F (–18°C), US zones 7–10.

Stachys 'Primrose Heron'

Valeriana phu 'Aurea'

Golden Hop at Barnsley House, Gloucestershire

Golden Feverfew

***Tanacetum parthenium* 'Aureum'**   A short-lived perennial with bright yellow green, finely divided leaves and white daisy flowers on stems to 1ft (30cm) in summer.

PLANTING HELP   Golden Feverfew will grow well in almost any moist soil, in sun or shade. It seeds itself around the garden and the seedlings come true. Hardy to −10°F (−23°C), US zones 6–9 or less.

Golden Lemon Balm *Melissa officinalis* 'Aurea'

Valeriana

***Valeriana phu* 'Aurea'**   A perennial which forms a clump of bright yellow young leaves in spring. The flowering stem grows to 5ft (1.5m) tall, producing insignificant white flowers, each less than ¼in (0.5cm) long, in summer.

PLANTING HELP   Grows in any moist or wet soil; useful in spring as a bright accent in a bog garden or in a shady spot under trees. Hardy to −10°F (−23°C), US zones 6–9.

Golden Feverfew *Tanacetum parthenium* 'Aureum'

Catalpa bignonioides 'Aurea'

Golden Catalpa

Catalpa bignonioides **'Aurea'** Indian Bean
Tree   A medium-sized tree to 40ft (12m) tall and
wide. The white flowers with purple markings are
never as fine as those of the green-leaved form.
The wild form is native to North America.

PLANTING HELP   Plant in autumn or early
spring; water well until established. Happy in any
soil but grows best in deep, fertile soil and full sun.
Hardy to −20°F (−29°C), US zones 5–10.

Golden False Acacia *Robinia pseudacacia* 'Frisia'

Golden Honey Locust

Gleditsia triacanthos **'Sunburst'** (syn. *Gleditsia
triacanthos* 'Inermis Aurea')   An elegant
deciduous spineless tree with weeping branches of
fern-like leaves; the young shoots and leaves are
yellow, but become green as they mature. In its
native North America *Gleditsia triacanthos* forms a
craggy tree to 160ft (45m), the small flowers and
shiny brown seed pods emerging from thick twigs
and bark, among clumps of vicious spines.
'Rubylace' has red young leaves.

PLANTING HELP   Plant in autumn or early
spring; water well until established. Tolerant of
poor soils and prefers full sun. Hardy to −40°F
(−40°C), US zones 3–10.

Golden False Acacia

Robinia pseudacacia **'Frisia'**   A very common
and conspicuous tree, the pinnate leaves
remaining bright yellowish green throughout the
summer and golden in autumn. It was first found
in Holland in 1935. The wild Robinia or False
Acacia, with its hanging bunches of scented white

Golden Honey Locust *Gleditsia triacanthos*
'Sunburst'

Quercus robur 'Concordia', a famous old tree at Wilton House, Wiltshire, England

pea flowers, is wild in E North America, where it can reach 90ft (27m).

PLANTING HELP   Plant in autumn or early spring; water well until established. Tolerant of poor soils and prefers full sun. Hardy to −40°F (−40°C), US zones 3–10.

Golden Oaks

Of the 600 or more species of oak, only a few have been found with golden leaves. They make very striking trees in spring when the young shoots are elongating, but they are even more liable to damage by late frosts than normal oaks, and they can also be damaged by hot sun.

PLANTING HELP   These grafted oaks are expensive to buy and slow to get established. Like all forest trees, they grow best when young in a sheltered glade, rather than in the middle of a field. In an exposed position, put protection around the tree for the first few years, and ensure that the soil is enriched with oak leaf-mould.

***Quercus rubra* 'Aurea'**   A small tree with bright yellow leaves in spring, becoming yellowish green in summer. The mature leaves are deeply lobed, the lobes ending in sharp points. The wild

Red Oak is a common forest tree in E North America, reaching a height of 160ft (45m). Hardy to −40°F (−40°C), US zones 3–10.

***Quercus robur* 'Concordia'**   A form of the English Oak with yellow leaves in spring, green suffused with yellow throughout the summer. Leaves have shallow, rounded lobes. A slow-growing tree to 40ft (12m) after around 100 years. First recorded in Belgium in 1843. Hardy to −10°F (−23°C), US zones 6–10.

Young leaves of *Quercus rubra* 'Aurea'

55

Sambucus racemosa 'Plumosa Aurea'

Berberis

Berberis is a large genus of over 500 species of spiny shrubs, found mainly in the Himalayas and South America. Many are excellent garden plants with attractive flowers or colourful fruit. Coloured foliage is found in the various forms of *Berberis thunbergii* from Japan, in the European *B. vulgaris* and in their hybrids. **Berberis thunbergii 'Aurea'** is a compact, spiny deciduous shrub to 2ft (60cm) tall and about as wide. The leaves are bright yellow in early summer, becoming pale green later. The small yellow flowers appear in spring, each about ⅓in (1cm) wide and in autumn the orange leaves and bright berries can be conspicuous.

PLANTING HELP   Plant in autumn or early spring in any good soil in full sun; water well until established. Hardy to −10°F (−23°C), US zones 6–10.

Berberis thunbergii 'Aurea'

Cornus

Cornus alba 'Aurea'   A spreading deciduous shrub to 10ft (3m), the leaves suffused with yellow, becoming extra-colourful in autumn. Bare stems red in winter; flowers small and white; fruits white. An easily grown shrub for a hedge or background planting.

Cornus alba 'Aurea' at Bressingham, Norfolk

PLANTING HELP   Plant in autumn or early spring in rich, moist soil; water well until established. Hardy to −40°F (−40°C), US zones 3–10.

Fuchsia

Fuchsia magellanica 'Aurea'   A golden-leaved form of the common hardy fuchsia, eventually reaching 10ft (3m) in mild areas, but usually grown as a low shrub, stems to 3⅓ft (1m) in a season. Leaves around 1in (2.5cm) long.

PLANTING HELP   Plant in spring or summer, in good, deep, fertile soil; in frosty areas make sure that the base of the plant is well below ground level, and it will behave as an herbaceous perennial. Water well until established. Hardy to 10°F (−12°C), US zones 8–10.

Spiraea japonica 'Goldflame'

Fuchsia magellanica 'Aurea' with purple beetroot at Levens Hall in Cumbria

Sambucus

Sambucus racemosa 'Plumosa Aurea'
A deciduous shrub that grows to 5ft (1.5m) tall
and wide. In spring it produces rounded heads of
small yellow flowers, each about ⅓in (1cm) wide.
The leaves have 5–7 deeply cut, golden leaflets,
which remain bright for most of the summer. The
wild green *Sambucus racemosa*, found wild in
N Europe and Asia, has beautiful red berries.

PLANTING HELP   Plant in autumn or early
spring in deep, rich, moist soil in a cool position;
water well until established. Hardy to −40°F
(−40°C), US zones 3–10.

Spiraea

Spiraea japonica 'Goldflame'   A very showy
deciduous shrub that grows to 5ft (1.5m) tall and
usually wider, with red-gold young shoots and
leaves. The flowers, which are not often formed,
are bright red, in a flat head. The leaves are
narrowly lanceolate and turn reddish-gold in
autumn.

PLANTING HELP   Plant in autumn or early
spring in sun or partial shade; water well until
established. Prune in spring to encourage strong
growth and good colour. Hardy to −20°F (−29°C),
US zones 5–10.

Golden Mock Orange

Philadelphus coronarius 'Aureus'
A deciduous shrub with bright yellow leaves that
gradually turn greener through the summer. It
grows to 7ft (2m) tall and wide, and in early
summer produces clusters of creamy white
flowers, each about 1in (2.5cm) wide, highly
scented like orange blossom.

PLANTING HELP   Plant in autumn or early
spring; water well until established. Happy in any
soil but grows best in deep, fertile soil and partial
shade will prevent the leaves becoming scorched
in hot sun. Hardy to −10°F (−23°C), US zones
6–10.

Golden Mock
Orange

Chamaesphacos ilicifolius

Setcreasea *Tradescantia pallida*, wild in C Mexico

Acaena

Acaena inermis **'Purpurea'**   A creeping, mat-forming perennial with purple leaves to 2¾in (7cm) long, made up of 11–15 toothed leaflets. Flowers insignificant, in round heads armed with red spines. The normal form has brownish or greyish leaves, and is found wild in New Zealand.

PLANTING HELP   Plant in spring or summer, in well-drained but peaty soil. Be careful that the plant is not overshadowed by stronger plants. Hardy to 10°F (−12°C), US zones 8–10.

Acaena inermis 'Purpurea' with *Geranium sessiliflorum* hybrid

Canna

Canna **'Wyoming'**   A large canna with stems to around 7ft (2m), purple leaves and orange-yellow flowers in late summer.

PLANTING HELP   Plant in spring or in early summer in cool areas, in good, deep, fertile soil; in frosty areas either lift the rhizomes and keep them indoors for the winter, or plant them deep and make sure that the base of the plant is protected from frost. Hardy to 32°F (0°C), US zones 10–11.

Chamaesphacos

Chamaesphacos ilicifolius   A spreading perennial like a dead-nettle, forming mats to 8in (20cm) high, with toothed purplish leaves and short spikes of tubular purple flowers in summer. This is the only species in the genus and is found wild in C Asia, Iran and Afghanistan.

PLANTING HELP   Plant in spring or summer, in good well-drained soil. Protect from winter wet in mild areas. Hardy to 10°F (−12°C), US zones 8–10.

Dahlia

Dahlia **'Bishop of Llandaff'**   A very distinct dahlia with deep purple leaves and bright scarlet semi-double flowers around 4in (10cm) across, in late summer. Stems usually to around 4ft (1.2m).

Dahlia 'Bishop of Llandaff'

Canna 'Wyoming'

tall. There are several other purple-leaved varieties, including one with single pink flowers and one with bronze double decorative flowers.

PLANTING HELP   Plant in spring or in early summer in cool areas, in good deep fertile soil; in frosty areas either lift the tubers and keep them indoors for the winter, or plant them deep and make sure that the base of the plant is protected from frost. Hardy to 32°F (0°C), US zones 10–11.

Geranium

***Geranium sessiliflorum* subsp. *novae-zealandiae* 'Nigricans'** × *Geranium traversii*
A miniature creeping and mat-forming geranium with silvery-purple leaves around ⅓in (1cm) across and small pale pink or white flowers ⅓in (1cm) across, on creeping stems. This unusual geranium is a hybrid between two species found wild in New Zealand. Hybrids with *Geranium sessiliflorum* 'Nigricans' have smaller, paler flowers from a central rosette of blackish leaves.

PLANTING HELP   Plant in spring or summer in well-drained soil; water in summer in dry weather. Hardy to 10°F (–12°C), US zones 8–10.

Setcreasea

Tradescantia pallida (syn. *Setcreasea purpurea*)
A rather fleshy perennial with stems to 1ft (30cm) long, with purple flat leaves 6in (15cm) long, around 1in (2.5cm) across. The small, 3-petalled, pale pink flowers appear in summer. We found this plant growing apparently wild on dry limestone rocks near Guanejuato in central Mexico. It is valuable for its purple leaves and extreme tolerance of drought, surviving for weeks without any water at all.

PLANTING HELP   Plant out in early summer, in a dry, sunny position, in shallow, sandy soil; it will grow well under the overhangs of eaves or other difficult places. In frosty areas bring the plant, or a piece of it, under cover for the winter. Hardy to 32°F (0°C), US zones 10–11.

Sedum telephium subsp. *maximum* 'Atropurpureum'

Lysimachia ciliata 'Firecracker'

Cimicifuga

Actaea simplex **'Brunette'** (syn, *Cimicifuga simplex*) A purplish-brown-leaved form of the common *Cimicifuga*, with dark brown leaves through the summer, and spikes to 4ft (1.2m) tall, of white flowers from purple buds in autumn.

PLANTING HELP Plant in early spring while dormant, in good leafy soil in partial shade, or in a mixed border. Propagate by division of the clumps in autumn or winter. Hardy to −20°F (−29°C), US zones 5–9.

Bronze Fennel

Foeniculum vulgare **'Purpureum'**
A decorative form of fennel with purplish bronze foliage which is valuable for its light and airy effect. The flowering stems, which can reach 7ft (2m) or more, are formed in midsummer. If the yellow flowers are not wanted, the flowering stems can be cut down when they appear.

PLANTING HELP Sow the seeds in well-drained soil where they are intended to flower and allow the plants to develop unchecked if possible. Hardy to 10°F (−12°C), US zones 8–10.

Heuchera

These evergreen or semi-evergreen perennials from North America have fleshy rootstocks which spread slowly into large clumps, providing good ground-cover. The tiny, bell-shaped, often red flowers rise on stems well above the circular leaves

which are hairy and sometimes beautifully tinted with grey, silver, pink or purple. Many new varieties have appeared in the past 5 years. *Heuchera* **'Plum Puddin'** is a variety with blackish-purple leaves around 3in (8cm) across, and airy sprays of very small, whitish flowers.

PLANTING HELP Plant in well-drained fertile soil in full sun or partial shade, sinking rootstocks well into the ground so that only the top of the foliage is visible. It is a good idea to divide and replant heucheras every few years, preferably in August or early September. Hardy to −20°F (−29°C), US zones 5–10.

Ligularia

Ligularia dentata **'Desdemona'** A large perennial forming robust clumps of rounded purplish leaves. In summer it produces clusters of yellow flower heads, 4in (10cm) wide, on dark purple-brown stems, to 4ft (1.2m) tall. The leaves are bronze-green above and a striking rich mahogany-red on the underside.

PLANTING HELP Plant in autumn or early spring, while dormant, in good leafy soil in partial shade, or a very moist bed in the sun. Propagate by division of the clumps in autumn or winter. Hardy to −20°F (−29°C), US zones 5–10.

Lysimachia

Lysimachia ciliata **'Firecracker'**
(syn. *Lysimachia ciliata* 'Purpurea') A perennial with creeping underground rhizomes and upright

Ligularia dentata 'Desdemona'

Young leaves of *Actaea simplex* 'Brunette'

Foeniculum vulgare 'Purpureum' at Iden Croft Herb Garden

stems to 4ft (1.2m) tall. Leaves and stems dark purple; flowers yellow. The normal green-leaved form is found wild in wet places throughout North America.

PLANTING HELP   Plant in autumn or early spring, while dormant, in good leafy soil in partial shade, or a very moist bed in the sun. Propagate by division in autumn or winter. Hardy to –40°F (–40°C), US zones 3–10.

Sedum

Sedum telephium subsp. *maximum* 'Atropurpureum'   A succulent perennial with fleshy stems and leaves that grows to 1½ft (45cm) tall. In summer and autumn it produces domed heads to 3in (8cm) wide, containing many flowers, each about ⅓in (1cm) wide. Best in a sunny position but not too dry in summer.

PLANTING HELP   For any good soil. Plant in spring and propagate by division. Water in dry summers, as these large-leaved sedums are not as drought-tolerant as the dwarf stonecrops. Hardy to 0°F (–18°C), US zones 7–10.

Heuchera 'Plum Puddin'

Red Japanese Maples at Drummond Castle Gardens, Scotland

Red Filbert *Corylus maxima* 'Purpurea'

Berberis

Berberis thunbergii 'Rose Glow'
A deciduous rounded shrub to 6ft (1.8m) in diameter, with round purple leaves, mottled and veined with pink when young. The small, yellow-purple backed flowers are followed by red berries. A commonly seen shrub, which is spectacular through the summer.

PLANTING HELP Plant in autumn or spring in any soil. Pruning in spring or summer encourages the growth of new pinkish shoots. Hardy to −20°F (−29°C), US zones 5–10.

Red Japanese Maples

Several varieties of Japanese maple (*Acer palmatum*) have red foliage in spring, becoming purple through the summer, followed by a good red in autumn. Named varieties such as 'Bloodgood' have particularly fine colour.

PLANTING HELP Plant in autumn or spring in good, leafy soil. Protect from hot sun and drying wind when young; water and mulch well in dry weather until established. Hardy to −20°F (−29°C), US zones 5–10.

Red Japanese Maple *Acer palmatum* f. *atropurpureum* A small, spreading deciduous tree 24ft (7m) tall. The reddish purple leaves become a beautiful vivid red in autumn. The wild green form is found in China, Korea and Japan.

Red Laceleaf Japanese Maple *Acer palmatum* 'Dissectum Nigrum' (syn. 'Ever Red') A low, rounded deciduous bush that grows into a mushroom shape about 5ft (1.5m) tall and as wide. The young leaves are covered with silky hairs and the deep reddish purple colour is retained throughout the summer.

Red Japanese Maple

Red Filbert

Corylus maxima
'Purpurea' A purple-leaved form of the common filbert which makes a large shrub around 8ft (2.5m) high and wide. The leaves remain dark purple through the summer; the long husks around the fruit are reddish. Found wild in E Europe and Turkey.

PLANTING HELP Plant in autumn or spring in any soil. Nut trees grow best in partial shade and shelter, and are slow to establish in open sites. Hardy to −20°F (−29°C), US zones 5–10.

Berberis thunbergii 'Rose Glow' with Purple Grape Vine *Vitis vinifera* 'Purpurea' at Levens Hall, Cumbria

Red Laceleaf Japanese Maple

Cotinus coggygria 'Notcutt's Variety'

Purple Smoke Bush

Cotinus coggygria 'Notcutt's Variety'
A deciduous shrub that grows to 15ft (4.5m) tall,
with pinkish grey and purple rounded leaves. In
late spring and early summer it produces large airy
clusters of misty flowers. The green-leaved species
is found wild in much of Europe and Asia from the
Mediterranean to the Himalayas and China.

PLANTING HELP   Plant in autumn or spring
in any soil. Prune hard in spring to encourage the
long upright shoots of colourful leaves shown
here. Grows well in areas with dry summers.
Hardy to 0°F (−18°C), US zones 7–10.

Purple Grape Vine

Vitis vinifera 'Purpurea'   A climber with
stems up to around 12ft (3.5m) in cultivation,
which can be kept in check by annual pruning. It
has lobed leaves around 6in (15cm) across; the
dark purple grapes are small and inedible. A good
foliage plant for a wall, or for flower arrangements;
it forms a fine background to anything pink, such
as the autumn-flowering nerines.

PLANTING HELP   Vines do best in deep,
moist, well-drained, preferably chalky soil, and are
best in full sun. Prune in winter. Hardy to 0°F
(−18°C), US zones 7–10.

Leaves of Globe Artichoke

Cynara

The genus *Cynara* consists of about three species of blue-flowered, thistle-like plants, from the Mediterranean area. It includes the well-known artichoke and the leafy cardoon.

PLANTING HELP   Cynara come from S Europe and N Africa where they grow in rather poor soil on dry, sunny slopes, but to reach a large size they need deep, well-drained soil, full sun, plenty of water and liberal applications of liquid fertilizer. Hardy to 10°F (–12°C), US zones 8–10, or less if protected with straw or fleece.

Cardoon *Cynara cardunculus*   This exotic-looking plant is similar to the artichoke (*see below*) and the leaf bases can be eaten when blanched, so it is often found in large kitchen gardens. Given the right conditions it will eventually reach a height of about 7ft (2m), and will need staking; it is best given a sheltered place if possible. It is also highly ornamental, and its huge leaves and purple, thistle-like flowers can look very good at the back of a summery mixed border.

Globe Artichoke *Cynara cardunculus* var. *scolymus*   This well-known vegetable is a smaller variety of the cardoon and has equally attractive leaves, but grows up to about 4ft (1.2m) or more in height. The artichokes themselves are also visually exciting, but only a gardener with supreme self-control will be able to resist eating them. Globe artichokes can be grown from seed, but better edible flowers will be had from offsets taken from a good plant.

Eryngium maritimum

Eryngium variifolium

Sea Hollies

Most species of *Eryngium* have particularly striking spiny leaves and cone-shaped flower heads surrounded by spiky bracts. They are good architectural plants, and have a long flowering season; some of them can be dried and brought indoors for flower arrangements in the winter.

PLANTING HELP   Eryngium can be grown from seed sown in spring and planted out in the autumn, or increased by taking root cuttings in late winter. They should be given a sunny place in ordinary, well-drained soil. Remember that most species are spiny, so avoid planting at the edges of paths and borders.

Eryngium bourgatii   This species comes from the Pyrenees and the Mediterranean east to Turkey, where it grows in dry rocky places, often on limestone. It is not one of the most common

Eryngium bourgatii

SILVER THISTLE-LIKE FOLIAGE

Cardoon *Cynara cardunculus* at Tapeley Park, near Bideford, Devon

sea hollies, but is becoming more widely available, and is well worth seeking out for its beautiful foliage. It grows up to about 2ft (60cm) high, and has deeply divided, curled, greyish-green leaves, silver-grey bracts and blue or silvery flower heads in midsummer. Hardy to 10°F (−12°C), US zones 8–10.

Eryngium giganteum As the name suggests, the true *Eryngium giganteum*, which is a native of N Turkey, Iran and the Caucasus, is a large plant, reaching up to about 4ft (1.2m) high when in flower, but the form known in gardens as 'Miss Wilmott's Ghost' is smaller, to 2ft (60cm). It has more or less heart-shaped green leaves, and silvery flower heads in late summer. It was named after Miss Ellen Wilmott, a famous and eccentric Edwardian gardener who is supposed to have scattered a few seeds of this plant in each of her friends' gardens when visiting, in the manner of a calling card. This Eryngium takes two seasons to flower and then dies, so you will need to plan ahead if you want flowers every summer. **'Silver Ghost'** is a taller, more silvery form, brought back by me from Turkey in 1980. Hardy to 10°F (−12°C), US zones 8–10.

Eryngium maritimum This is the true sea holly, which is found growing on the beaches of W Europe, including Britain, the Mediterranean and the Black Sea. In the wild it grows on sand dunes, but it also does well in deep, well-drained sandy soil in the garden, thriving in hot, dry conditions. This is a low-growing species, which

makes a wide clump and reaches a height of about 1ft (30cm). The leathery leaves are silvery green, with large, triangular, spiny teeth, and spiny bracts surround the greyish blue flowers, which appear from June to September. Hardy to 10°F (−12°C), US zones 8–10.

Eryngium variifolium This ferocious plant comes from damp places in the mountains of Morocco. It makes a rosette of round, evergreen leaves with conspicuous white veins. The rounded blue flower heads with whitish bracts are borne from June to August on stiff, greyish-white stems. Does well in short grass or good moist soil in full sun. Hardy to 10°F (−12°C), US zones 8–10.

Eryngium giganteum
'Silver Ghost'

Artemisia

Artemisia are some of the best grey-leaved perennials for the garden. They are mostly tough and easy to grow, which partly accounts for their popularity, but their leaves are also extremely attractive, and provide a good foil for green-leaved plants. They are true foliage plants in the sense that the leaves are far more striking than the flowers. Some people cut the flowers off so as not to detract from the beauty of the plant.

PLANTING HELP   Most Artemisia like well-drained, dryish soil and full sun; some kinds, such as **'Powis Castle'** do well and look good if they are planted on top of a wall or raised bed so that they can hang down over the edge. Perennial plants can be divided and replanted during the winter, while the shrubby species can be increased by taking cuttings in August and growing on through the winter in a cold frame, before planting

out once the weather is milder. 'Powis Castle', in particular, is not always reliably hardy, so it is wise to take a few cuttings each year as a precaution.

Wormwood *Artemisia absinthium*   A native of Europe and N Africa, where it grows in a wide range of places and flowers throughout the summer. Illustrated here is **'Lambrook Silver'**, a form selected by the British gardener Margery Fish, and named after her garden in Somerset. It makes an attractive deciduous shrubby plant up to 2½ft (75cm) and has grey, finely divided leaves and long branched spikes of small greyish yellow flowers. Another

Artemisia stelleriana 'Mori's Form'

Artemisia arborescens 'Powis Castle' in a dry, sunny bed at Powis Castle

Artemisia absinthium 'Lambrook Silver'

Artemisia alba 'Canescens' at Cockermouth Castle, Cumbria

similar, but larger form, 'Lambrook Giant' is also available. All forms benefit from being cut hard back in the spring. Hardy to 10°F (−12°C), US zones 7–10.

***Artemisia alba* 'Canescens'**   This is a rather weird-looking plant, with its curling, lacy silver-grey leaves, but it has proved popular with gardeners, and is easy to grow in a sunny place as long as the soil is well-drained. This plant is fairly low-growing, and makes good ground-cover, although it sends out flower stems up to about 1½ft (45cm). Hardy to −10°F (−23°C), US zones 6–9.

***Artemisia arborescens* 'Powis Castle'**
Perhaps the best known of all Artemisia, this makes a wonderful silver-grey clump. Named after Powis Castle, Powys, Wales, and seen to great effect there where it tumbles over the walls like a waterfall. It is a quick-growing perennial, but can also form a shrub in mild areas, although it is unlikely to survive a really cold, wet winter in Britain; it does best in poor, well-drained soil, since very wet conditions cause the stems to rot. Hardy to 20°F (−6°C), US zones 9–10.

***Artemisia ludoviciana* 'Silver Queen'**   This is a selection of one of the more hardy species from North America. It grows to 3ft (90cm) with narrow, willow-like leaves and insignificant little flowers in mid- to late summer. It spreads by running roots. Hardy to −20°F (−29°C), US zones 5–10.

***Artemisia stelleriana* 'Mori's Form'** (syn. 'Boughton Silver')   A low-growing Japanese perennial which appreciates sandy soils and full sun. The leaves are whitish grey and deeply divided. Hardy to 0°F (−18°C), US zones 7–10.

African Sage

Salvia aethiopis A perennial or biennial, forming wide rosettes of large, felted leaves and sending up flowering stems to about 2ft (60cm). Our picture shows just how good the leaves look in contrast with the narrower ones of the Artemisia. Despite its name, it is native of C and S Europe and W Asia.

PLANTING HELP   Does well in similar conditions to those required by Artemisia, a sunny position in light, well-drained soil, sandy if possible. Seed can be sown outside in the place where you want it, but remember that it will take two years to flower, and that it will need plenty of room! Hardy to 0°F (−18°C), US zones 7–10.

Artemisia ludoviciana 'Silver Queen'

African Sage and *Artemisia ludoviciana* at the Royal Botanic Garden, Edinburgh

Brachyglottis 'Sunshine' in Eccleston Square, London   *Tanacetum densum* subsp. *amani*

Brachyglottis

Brachyglottis 'Sunshine' (formerly called *Senecio greyi*)   An evergreen which forms a rather lax bush up to about 3ft (90cm) tall, sometimes used to make a low hedge in exposed places. The dull green leaves are covered underneath with masses of greyish-white hairs, giving an attractive felted effect; the yellow, daisy-like flowers appear in early summer. It is a common and really good, tough garden plant, and very easy to grow. *Brachyglottis* (formerly included in *Senecio*) is a genus of a few species of shrubby daisies, native of the South Island of New Zealand. **B. monroi** has leaves which are oblong with wavy edges, mid-green on the upper side, greyish white underneath. *Brachyglottis compacta* is a rarer dwarf species. All are especially useful for coastal planting, as they are wind- and salt-tolerant.

PLANTING HELP   Propagate by taking cuttings in late summer and keeping in a cold frame over the winter. Pot on during the spring and the plants will be ready to plant outside in the following autumn. In cold areas plant out in spring. Hardy to 10°F (−12°C), US zones 8–10.

Senecio

Senecio cineraria 'Silver Dust' (syn. *Senecio candicans, Senecio maritima*)   This is an almost hardy evergreen species, but, coming as it does from the Mediterranean region it is often treated as a half-hardy annual. It makes a plant up to about 2ft (60cm) high and roughly half as wide. There are several forms available, but the one we show here is particularly good, with very deeply divided, white-felted leaves which make a good show for much of the year. The small yellow flowers appear during the summer but are not particularly interesting, and are often removed.

Brachyglottis monroi

Senecio cineraria 'Silver Dust'

Stachys byzantina at Crathes Castle, Deeside

Tanacetum

Tanacetum densum* subsp. *amani A low-growing perennial which forms dense mats of silver leaves and has clusters of minute yellow flowers in midsummer. Wild in rocky places in Turkey. Very easy to grow in the right conditions.

PLANTING HELP This is good on dry walls, or in raised beds or other well-drained sites in poor, stony soil in sun or light shade. In common with many other silver-leaved plants it will not tolerate waterlogging, but otherwise requires little care. The plants can be divided and replanted in the spring. Hardy to 10°F (−12°C), US zones 8–10.

Anthemis

Anthemis punctata* subsp. *cupaniana
A lovely perennial daisy from Sicily, where it grows on cliffs and in rocky places, making it very suitable for the edges of paths and raised beds. It forms dense mats of finely divided, silvery grey leaves, and also bears very attractive, large, white, daisy-like flowers throughout the summer and into the autumn.

PLANTING HELP This is easy to grow on poor, well-drained soil in a sunny place; dead-heading will result in a long season of contrasting flowers and foliage. The plants can be divided and replanted in the spring. Hardy to 10°F (−12°C), US zones 8–10, for short periods.

PLANTING HELP This plant is easy to grow, in well-drained, preferably slightly sandy soil in full sun, being especially useful in pots and containers. Unless you are very keen, we would suggest buying young plants rather than trying to propagate them from seed, which requires heat. Hardy to 20°F (−6°C), US zones 9–10.

Stachys

Stachys byzantina (syn. *Stachys lanata*) Rabbits Ears or Lambs Ears A well-known garden plant, this is loved by small children for its wonderfully soft, silky grey leaves, hence the common names. Adults, too, find it attractive at the front of a border or as edging for paths, and it is very easy to grow. It is low-growing, forming spreading mats of leaves, but the pink flowers are borne on stems which rise to about 3ft (90cm). There are several distinct forms available, such as that shown here, with variegated leaves.

PLANTING HELP As it is native to rocky places in Turkey (hence the name *byzantina*), the Caucasus mountains and Iran, this species likes hot, dry, sunny places and well-drained soil if possible (although it always seems to do perfectly well in ordinary garden soils too). The plants can be dug up, the roots pulled apart and replanted during the autumn and spring. Hardy to 0°F (−18°C), US zones 7–10.

Anthemis punctata subsp. *cupaniana*

Centaurea argentea at Wisley

Centaurea

Centaurea argentea A lovely, hardy perennial from Crete, where it grows on mountain rocks and in gorges, which makes it suitable for dry walls in gardens. This knapweed grows up to about 18in (45cm) high, with divided, silvery leaves and yellow flower heads borne singly on stalks in summer.

PLANTING HELP One of the most uncommon plants in this book, but worth looking out for at sales of rare plants (often organized by members of local societies). Once you have tracked down a plant, give it a dry, sunny place in well-drained soil on a wall, protect from damp in winter and enjoy the superb foliage. Propagation is by seed in spring or by division in spring or autumn. Hardy to 10°F (–12°C), US zones 8–10.

Rue

Ruta graveolens A common shrubby herb, which was used for cooking in the past, but is now generally grown solely for its attractive foliage. It makes a compact plant, up to about 3ft (90cm) tall, with aromatic, deeply divided greyish green leaves. Clusters of small yellow flowers appear in early summer. The variety 'Jackman's Blue', which is widely available, has rather bluer leaves and makes a more compact plant, usually up to about 2ft (60cm) at the most.

PLANTING HELP Plants can be set out from autumn to spring in sunny places in well-drained soil. After the first year trim back to the old wood to prevent legginess, and dead-head in the autumn. Propagate by seed sown in spring, growing the plants on in a cold frame until the weather warms up, when they can be potted on and put outside, before planting in the autumn. **Warning:** be careful when handling this plant as the milky juice can cause severe irritation in some people – always wear gloves. Hardy to 10°F (–12°C), US zones 8–10.

Garden Pink 'Mrs Sinkins'

Garden Pinks

In contrast to *Centaurea*, pinks are some of the commonest perennial plants you can find. Given the right conditions, they are rewarding and easy to grow, and valued for their sweet-smelling flowers. Once dead-headed, the leaves of pinks can also be enjoyed, and some will reward you with compact mounds of foliage until late in the autumn. Those we particularly recommend for their leaves are 'Bat's Double Red', an old variety with double, deep red flowers and exceptionally

Ruta graveolens

good glaucous foliage; **'Mrs Sinkins'**, an old but exceptionally vigorous variety with untidy flowers, usually with a split cayyx and exceptionally good scent; White Ladies' is similar, with neater white flowers and even greyer foliage.

PLANTING HELP All pinks do best in sunny conditions in well-drained soil; they are particularly suited to raised beds and make good plants for the edges of paths. The older varieties do well with very little attention, whereas the modern varieties often benefit from having their tips pinched out, to encourage bushy growth. Very few varieties will tolerate waterlogging – this, combined with very low winter temperatures will kill them. Most pinks will need replacing after three or four years, as they tend to become woody and straggly. Easily propagated by means of cuttings, with three or four pairs of leaves, taken at flowering time. Hardy to 0°F (−18°C), US zones 7–10.

Lotus

Lotus berthelotii An elegant, shrubby plant for warm gardens only, with long, trailing stems bearing fine, ferny, silvery grey leaves. The claw-like flowers, to about 1in (2.5cm) in length, are red, orange or yellow, and are produced in spring and early summer. This makes an excellent foliage plant for pots and window boxes, but will not withstand very low temperatures.

PLANTING HELP Needs a position in full sun, in well-drained but moisture-retentive soil. Bring inside in winter, or take cuttings in summer. Hardy to 32°F (0°C), US zones 10–11.

Stock

White Perennial Stock *Matthiola incana* This form of the wild stock lives for up to 5 years, and makes a very satisfactory clump of grey leaves on a stout, woody stem, eventually up to about 3ft (90cm). It has numerous white, powerfully scented flowers, which, if dead-headed, will go on looking good throughout the summer, and the foliage continues to please until the autumn.

PLANTING HELP This stock does well in a sunny place in well-drained, sandy soil. It needs little care, and given half a chance will seed itself all over the place, so it is easy to obtain new plants; you can also collect the seed in autumn from the ripe pods and sow it in the spring. Hardy to 10°F (−12°C), US zones 8–10.

Lotus berthelotii in a tall herb pot   White Perennial Stock *Matthiola incana*

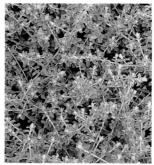

Santolina pinnata
subsp. neapolitana

Plecostachys serpyllifolia

Helichrysum splendidum

Cistus

Cistus albidus An evergreen shrub, to 4ft
(1.2m), although it can be kept more compact
than this in the garden. The soft leaves are grey;
the flowers (which appear in late spring) pink,
with a spot of yellow at the base. There is also a
form with white flowers. Native of SW Europe.

PLANTING HELP All *Cistus* like full sun and
well-drained conditions; they are particularly
suited to growing on dry banks or in areas with
poor, stony soil. They can be cut back lightly in the
spring to remove dead wood, but otherwise
require little attention. Hardy to 10°F (−12°C),
US zones 8–10 if kept dry.

Convolvulus

The two species of *Convolvulus* described here are
very different from one another, and with the
exception of the flowers, neither of them really
look like the common bindweed or like the related
Morning Glory.

PLANTING HELP Good for well-drained soil
in a sunny place (it will also tolerate light shade).
The roots are inclined to be invasive, so it is useful
to restrain it by planting at the
edges of paths or terraces,
where it cannot
rampage through other
plants. Increase by
digging up pieces of
root and replanting
where required. Hardy to
20°F (−6°C), US zones 9–10

Convolvulus althaeoides
A trailing or climbing
perennial, with slender stems
up to 3½ft (1m), greyish
green, finely divided leaves
and pink flowers.

Convolvulus
althaeoides

Convolvulus cneorum An excellent small
evergreen shrub for the grey border, this forms a
clump up to about 18in (45cm), with narrow grey
leaves, and bindweed-like white flowers striped
with pink on the outside. Given the right
conditions it is a tough plant, which will give form
to your border after lesser plants have died away.
Hardy to 20°F (−6°C) US zones 9–10, in a
sheltered place.

Santolina chamaecyparissus

PLANTING HELP This Mediterranean native likes well-drained poor soil and full sun, and heartily dislikes waterlogging. It grows best in a crevice in a dry, sunny wall. Propagate by taking cuttings in late summer.

Convolvulus cneorum

Helichrysum

This is a huge group of annuals, shrubs and perennials, some of which are grown for their straw-like 'everlasting' flowers, and others for their foliage. Popular plants, other than those illustrated, include the well-known Curry Plant *Helichrysum italicum* (syn. *Helichrysum angustifolium*) with narrow, silvery grey leaves, which smell strongly of curry, and *H. petiolare* 'Limelight' and 'Variegatum', which are tender trailing plants much used in pots and containers.

PLANTING HELP Helichrysums like well-drained soil and a sunny position. Cut *Helichrysum splendidum* back hard in spring to keep the plant compact, and trim over again in early summer to keep the leaves looking good. Take cuttings in late summer.

Helichrysum splendidum A native of Africa, this is an evergreen shrub to 3½ft (1m), with silvery white leaves covered with masses of tiny hairs, giving a woolly effect. The heads of small, bright yellow flowers are borne at the tips of the shoots throughout the summer, but are often cut off so as not to detract from the effect of the foliage. Hardy to 20°F (–6°C), US zones 9–11.

Plecostachys serpyllifolia (syn. *Helichrysum serpyllifolium*) A lax shrub, to 5ft (1.5m), with stiff stems and very small, white furry leaves. The small insignificant white flowers appear in spring. Hardy to 20°F (–6°C), US zones 9–11.

Cotton Lavender

Santolina is a genus of low-growing, evergreen shrubs, with finely divided, aromatic leaves and tiny, bright yellow flowers in button-like heads in summer.

PLANTING HELP As with many other Mediterranean plants, these need a sunny place in well-drained soil; they are good as edging plants, or can be used to make a low hedge. A good trim back in the early summer will help to prevent any tendency to legginess. Cuttings can be taken in summer. Hardy to 10°F (–12°C), US zones 8–11.

Santolina chamaecyparissus This makes a mound to about 2ft (60cm), with narrow, silvery grey leaves.

Santolina pinnata subsp. *neapolitana* (syn. *Santolina tomentosa*) A slightly more lax plant, but similar in height to *Santolina chamaecyparissus*, this has longer, more feathery leaves and slightly paler yellow flowers.

Cistus albidus

Ballota

Ballota pseudodictamnus A low-growing shrubby perennial, to about 18in (45cm), commonly used as a bedding plant in pots and containers. The felted, yellowish-grey green leaves are almost heart-shaped; the small white flowers appear in summer, but are insignificant. A native of the Greek Islands, where it grows on rocky rough ground.

PLANTING HELP Best planted out in spring in a sunny place, in well-drained soil. In wet areas they will need protection with cloches or bell jars, but it is probably best to raise new plants. Take cuttings of non-flowering shoots in late summer, and overwinter in a mixture of peat and sand in a cold frame; plant out in the garden the following spring. Hardy to 20 °F (–6°C), US zones 9–10, or less if protected from excessive winter wet.

Lavender

***Lavandula* 'Princess Blue'** A good, tall variety with stems around 1ft (30cm) from the uppermost leaves, and a flowering head around 2¾in (7.5cm) long, in autumn. Flowers pale lavender-blue. Hardy to about 10°F (–12°C), US zones 8–10.

Lavandula 'Princess Blue' at Quince House, Devon

PLANTING HELP All lavenders need well-drained soil and a sunny position in the garden. The hardy species and varieties are easy to grow, provided they do not become waterlogged in the winter, and will give several years of pleasure if kept trimmed back after flowering. If your plants show signs of becoming leggy give them a hard cut back in early April to promote new growth. To obtain replacement plants, simply take cuttings from non-flowering shoots in August and overwinter (in a cold frame if you have one) in a mix of sand and peat; they can then be put out in the garden the following spring.

Hebe pinguifolia 'Red Edge'

Dorycnium

Lotus hirsutus (syn. *Dorycnium hirsutum*) A very low-growing evergreen shrub to only about 2in (5cm) tall, with a woody base and branching annual stems clothed with numerous small, grey-green leaves covered with white hairs. The flower heads appear in midsummer, and are made up of 6–10 tiny white or pink pea flowers, which are followed by red seed pods in autumn.

PLANTING HELP Easy to grow in light, even poor, well-drained soil in full sun. Propagate from seed collected from the seed pods and sown in spring. Hardy to 10°F (–12°C), US zones 8–10.

Dorycnium *Lotus hirsutus*

Hebe

Hebe pinguifolia 'Red Edge' This is a selection of a species from New Zealand with purplish stems and good clumps of grey leaves edged with red. To about 1ft (30cm) or more tall, making an excellent plant for the front of a border.

PLANTING HELP Good in well-drained soil in a sunny place. Can be easily increased by taking cuttings from the numerous non-flowering shoots in late summer, and growing on in a mixture of sand and peat; no heat needed. Hardy to 10°F (−12°C), US zones 8–10.

Ballota pseudodictamnus

Purple Honeywort

Cerinthe major 'Pupurascens'
A native of S Europe, this annual is a rather sinister-looking plant with bluish green leaves and bluish black bracts from which arise nodding clusters of tubular yellow and purple flowers in late spring and summer. It sends up stems to about 2ft (60cm) tall.

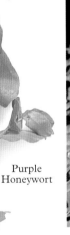

Purple Honeywort

PLANTING HELP This is easy to grow and can be raised from seed sown in spring in ordinary, fairly well-drained soil where it is to flower. Hardy to 10°F (−12°C), US zones 8–10.

Phlomis italica

Jerusalem Sage

Phlomis are shrubs and herbaceous perennials from the Mediterranean east to Kashmir.

PLANTING HELP These do well in full sun, in dry, well-drained soil. Take cuttings in early autumn and overwinter in a mix of peat and sand in a cold frame or unheated greenhouse. Hardy to 10°F (−12°C), US zones 8–10.

Phlomis fruticosa A low-growing, evergreen shrub to 3.5ft (1m) or more with softly felted whitish grey leaves and yellow flowers in early summer.

Phlomis italica A herbaceous perennial, also has beautiful foliage and pale pink flowers. A native of the Mediterranean region, where it grows on cliffs and rocky limestone hills.

Jerusalem Sage *Phlomis fruticosa* in Greece

Young shoots of *Macleya cordata*

Parahebe perfoliata

Hosta 'Blue Danube'

Dicentra

Dicentra 'Silver Beads' A perennial forming compact patches with creeping rhizomes, with silvery, ferny leaves. The hanging flowers produced throughout summer are ¾in (2cm) long, whitish, with swollen outer petals. 'Silver Smith' is similar; 'Langtrees' is less silvery.

PLANTING HELP   Plant in spring in moist but well-drained soil, growing well on shaded rock outcrops, or under trees. Hardy to 0°F (−18°C), US zones 7–10.

Blue Fescue

Festuca glauca 'Elijah Blue' This low-growing, evergreen grass has fine, blue-grey leaves, and makes hummocks up to 1ft (30cm). It is a tough and useful perennial for the front of borders, a striking change of shape from other foliage plants. There are several named varieties available, of which 'Caesia' and 'Elijah Blue' are particularly good.

PLANTING HELP   Plants tend to die off in the centre after a few years; to keep them in good shape, split up and replant every third spring or so. Easily grown in ordinary, well-drained soil in a sunny place. Do not allow other plants to overshadow the clumps. Hardy to −10°F (−23°C), US zones 6–10.

Blue Hostas

Many hostas have striking blue-grey foliage. These tend to be more tolerant of sun than the green-leaved varieties, though their colour develops best in some shade. They vary in size from the very large *Hosta sieboldiana* 'Elegans' to the small 'Halcyon' and 'Sherborne Swift'.

PLANTING HELP   Plant hostas in autumn or early spring in deep, rich, leafy soil in partial shade, or full sun in cloudy areas. Protect from slugs and snails, especially when the leaves are young. Most hostas are hardy to −40°F (−40°C), US zones 3–10, but in cold areas should be well mulched in autumn.

Hosta 'Blue Danube' A mound-forming perennial that grows to 2ft (60cm) across. The leaves are blue-green, and the violet, bell-shaped flowers appear at midsummer.

Hosta sieboldiana 'Elegans' One of the commonest hostas in the wild, this plant forms a magnificent clump of heavily puckered,

Blue *Hosta sieboldiana* 'Elegans' with the pale green of *Aruncus dioicus*

sumptuous, blue grey green leaves around 14in (35cm) long. Pale violet flowers on short stems are produced in July. Prefers light shade to three-quarters sun.

Macleya

Macleya cordata A tall perennial for the back of a large border, with rounded and scalloped greyish leaves, and stems to 7ft (2m) or more in late summer, with small, whitish or pink flowers around ½in (1.5cm) long, with long stamens. Found wild in Japan and E China, in forest clearings.

PLANTING HELP   Plant in autumn or early spring in deep, rich, leafy soil in partial shade, or full sun in cloudy areas. The rhizomes run underground and the plant can soon form large patches. Hardy to −40°F (−40°C), US zones 3–10.

Parahebe

Parahebe perfoliata A trailing evergreen perennial with stems to 2½ft (75cm) long, and perfoliate leaves around 2in (5cm) across. The small, blue flowers are in slender spikes from among the leaves in summer. Found wild in SE Australia.

PLANTING HELP   Plant in spring in well-drained soil in full sun or partial shade in hot areas. Hardy to 20°F (−6°C), US zones 9–11, or the warmer parts of zone 8.

Dicentra 'Silver Beads'

Blue Fescue *Festuca glauca* 'Elijah Blue'

77

Buddleja

Buddleja crispa   There are many beautiful
buddlejas available, but one of the very best for
foliage is this large, bushy, deciduous shrub, which
comes from the Himalayas and Afghanistan. It
normally grows up to about 6ft (1.8m) in gardens,
but can reach up to double that height, making a
small tree. It has downy, greyish green leaves, to
about 4½in (12cm) long and fragrant, lilac flower
heads from early summer into late autumn.

PLANTING HELP   Easy to grow in good
garden soil, and in cooler climates does best when
grown against a wall. Can be propagated by
cuttings taken in late summer. Hardy to −10°F
(−23°C), US zones 6–9.

Rose

Rosa glauca (syn. *Rosa rubrifolia*)
A large shrub to 13ft (4m) with arching
branches and lovely grey or purplish foliage. The
small, slightly scented, pale pink flowers appear in
summer, and are followed in autumn by numerous
bright red hips. Native of mountainous areas of
Europe, from the Pyrenees to Albania.

PLANTING HELP   Best in reasonably fertile,
moist soil in sun or light shade. Avoid planting in
ground that has previously had roses in it. Hardy
to −30°F (−35°C), US zones 4–8.

Sea Buckthorn

Hippophae rhamnoides   A deciduous rounded
shrub or tree to 33ft (10m) in the wild, but usually
much less in gardens. The narrow leaves are a

beautiful soft silver-grey, and the
tiny flowers insignificant, but if
both sexes are planted together
there is a bonus of orange
berries in autumn and
winter. Native of Europe
(including Britain)
and Asia.

PLANTING HELP
Fast-growing plants
which will do best in a
sunny place on poor,
sandy, well-drained soil.
Propagation is by seed,
which should be
collected and sown
when ripe (late
summer) in seed
compost and kept
over winter in a cold
frame. The seedlings
will need to be
pricked out and
grown on for a couple
of years before being large enough to plant out.
Hardy to −10°F (−23°C), US zones 6–9.

Sea
Buckthorn

Oleaster

Elaeagnus 'Quicksilver'   A large deciduous
shrub, to 10ft (3m) tall, with oval silvery leaves,
probably a hybrid between *Elaeagnus angustifolia*
and *E. commutata*. Flowers insignificant, but very
sweetly scented, small, bell-shaped, with 4 pointed
petals, in early summer. There are over 40 species
of these evergreen or deciduous shrubs, mainly
from Asia, although *E. commutata* is native to

Buddleja crispa

Rosa glauca at Gravetye Manor, Sussex

North America. Here we illustrate the one with the best silvery grey foliage; the variegated evergreen forms are described on page 25. *Elaeagnus angustifolia* makes a large deciduous shrub or small tree to about 12ft (3.5m) tall and almost as wide. The young branches are white and bear narrow, willow-like leaves which are silvery beneath, green above. The heavily scented, small silvery flowers appear in early summer and are followed by orange edible fruits. Wild throughout much of Asia, and commonly planted in North America. The American *Elaeagnus commutata* is a slower-growing spreading deciduous shrub to about 6ft (1.8m). The reddish brown stems bear silvery-grey leaves and creamy silvery flowers in spring, followed by edible grey fruits.

PLANTING HELP   An excellent shrub for exposed places and particularly good by the sea, as it is salt tolerant; it will do well in ordinary or sandy soil. Propagate by removing rooted suckers. Hardy to −40°F (−40°C), US zones 3–8.

Willow-leaved Pear

***Pyrus salicifolia* 'Pendula'**   This is a small tree, to about 20ft (6m) high, with pendulous branches and silvery grey-green, willow-like leaves, covered when young with fine white hairs. As the summer wears on, the leaves lose their silvery-white covering and become plain dark green. Small white flowers are produced in April, and these are followed by pear-like fruits (not good to eat). 'Pendula' is a cultivated form of *Pyrus salicifolia* which is a native of Russia, Turkey and Iran.

PLANTING HELP   A tough plant, easy to grow in any ordinary garden soil. Not easy to propagate; you are hardly likely to need more than one or two, so content yourself with buying plants from your local nursery or garden centre. Hardy to −40°F (−40°C), US zones 3–8.

Oleaster *Elaeagnus* 'Quicksilver'

Oleaster *Elaeagnus* 'Quicksilver'

Willow-leaved Pear

Willow-leaved Pear in the white garden at Sissinghurst

Decorative herbs & vegetables

Many herbs and vegetables are highly ornamental, and can be enjoyed either in the kitchen garden or planted in the mixed border. Some are actually bred for their looks (ornamental kale, for example) whereas others, such as ordinary Florence fennel, look wonderful anyway. We illustrate a small selection here to whet your appetite, but you will find many more in the pages of seed catalogues.

Fennel *Foeniculum vulgare*

Common Sage

Salvia officinalis   Sage is a shrubby herb, to about 2ft (60cm) tall, commonly grown for culinary use, but there are several forms with particularly good foliage which can be also used to good effect in the pleasure garden. Two we have found to be robust and easy to grow are 'Icterina', a variegated form; and **'Purpurascens'**, with purple and grey leaves.

PLANTING HELP   Best in good, well-drained soil, in a sunny sheltered place in the garden, or in a pot which can be brought indoors if the weather turns very cold. Trim the plant back after flowering every year to avoid it becoming straggly, although after about five years it will become woody and need replacing. Sage is quite easy to propagate by layering, by division or by taking cuttings from young shoots in late spring and growing them on in pots outside. Hardy to about 0°F (–18°C), US zones 7–10, unless they are waterlogged.

Rhubarb Chard

Golden Bay

Salvia officinalis 'Purpurascens'

Beet & Chard

Ornamental Beets *Beta vulgaris*
The humble beetroots and chards seldom stray from the vegetable garden, but our illustration shows how they can be used to great effect in a formal planting scheme. Two good varieties of beetroot with purple leaves include **'MacGregor's Favourite'**, an old Scottish variety, and 'Bull's Blood', which is similar, but with broader leaves. **Rhubarb Chard** *Beta vulgaris* subsp. *cicla* can be grown to great effect in formal kitchen gardens and grand potagers, such as Villandry in France. There are several varieties available from seedsmen with leaf stalks of different hues, for example 'Rainbow Chard', with yellow, orange and red stalks. Both are treated as annuals, so hardiness is irrelevant.

PLANTING HELP   Beetroot and chard do well in light, well-drained soil that has not been recently manured. Seed can be sown in February or March, and the plants thinned out to about 6in (15cm) apart. These ornamental varieties are perfectly edible.

Golden Bay

Laurus nobilis **'Aurea'**   If left to their own devices, ordinary green bay trees make shrubs or trees up to 65ft (20m) tall, but in a smallish garden this is often not possible, so they are trimmed into formal shapes. The golden-leaved form shown here can also be trimmed to shape, and used as a contrast plant in a border, or as a specimen shrub in a pot (when young).

PLANTING HELP   Bay is not easy to propagate and large, trained plants are usually expensive to buy, so purchase a small plant from the herb section of nurseries and garden centres that is about 1ft (30cm) tall then grow it on and train it yourself. Although slow to start with, once planted out in a sunny, sheltered place in good, well-drained garden soil, it will take off, and you will soon find it needs a good trim every year to prevent it from become straggly. Hardy to about 10°F (−12°C), US zones 8–10 in a sheltered site. Prolonged hard frosts may kill the upper growth, but it will usually sprout again from the base in spring.

Fennel

Foeniculum vulgare   This is grown for its edible roots, leaves and seeds, but it also looks very good at the back of a mixed border, its feathery leaves contrasting well with many broad-leaved plants. There is also a form with bronze leaves.

PLANTING HELP   Fennel does well in light, well-drained soil, but also requires plenty of water and a cool growing season to form good bulbs. Seed can be sown directly outside in spring or early summer, with the young plants thinned to about 18in (45cm) apart so as to allow plenty of room for the foliage. Hardy to 10°F (−12°C), US zones 8–10.

Purple beetroot with box edging and golden fuchsias at Levens Hall, Cumbria

Hosta fortunei 'Spinners' at the Savill Garden, Windsor

Hostas

Hostas are good, perennial plants, available in a huge range of colours; shown here are some of those with variegated leaves. Their young leaves are particularly delicate, and they are best planted in the shade where they are good for lighting up a dark corner.

PLANTING HELP   Plant in autumn or early spring in deep, rich, leafy soil in partial shade, or full sun in cloudy areas. Leaf colours develop best in full light, but hot sun will scorch the leaves. Protect from slugs and snails, especially when the leaves are young. Most hostas are hardy to −40°F (−40°C), US zones 3–10, but in cold areas should be well mulched in autumn.

Hosta **'Brim Cup'**   To 1ft (30cm) high and about 1½ft (45cm) across, with roundish leaves, mid-green in the centre, but surrounded by a wide cream margin. The flowers are whitish.

Hosta fortunei **'Albomarginata'**   This makes a clump to about 1½ft (45cm) tall, with greyish green leaves edged with white. It bears lavender coloured flowers in July. This is a good plant for autumn interest as it keeps its colour until the first frost.

Hosta fortunei var. *albopicta*   This makes a clump to about 2ft (60cm) high and wide, with striking, bright yellow leaves edged with pale green in spring. As the summer wears on, the yellow gradually fades, becoming pale green, and the green margin becomes darker. The trumpet-shaped, pale lilac flowers are held aloft on elegant stalks from mid- to late summer.

Hosta fortunei **'Spinners'**   A form making a medium-sized clump of green leaves with a wide, irregular white margin. Previously known as 'Alba Aurea', but named after his nursery in the New Forest by Peter Chappell.

Hosta sieboldiana **'Frances Williams'**   This makes a large clump, to about 2½ft (75cm) or more high and wide, with large leaves up to 1ft (30cm) long and wide. These are bluish grey, with strongly marked yellow edges, which deepen in colour through the summer. The flowers are white, flushed with lilac and appear just above the leaves in midsummer. Named after the owner of an American nursery, although it was previously sold under the name 'Gold Edge'.

Hosta montana **'Aureo-marginata'**   To 2ft (60cm) or more tall, and rather wider, bearing large, rich green leaves with a distinct wide golden edge and densely grouped, pale lavender flowers in late midsummer.

'Frances Williams'

Hosta montana 'Aureo-marginata' at Wisley

Hosta fortunei 'Albomarginata'

Hosta fortunei var. *albopicta*

Hosta sieboldiana 'Frances Williams'

Hosta 'Brim Cup'

Astrantia major 'Sunningdale Variegated'

Astrantia

***Astrantia major* 'Sunningdale Variegated'**
All the astrantias are attractive, but this form is
particularly good as a foliage plant. It makes a
clump to about 2ft (60cm) high, with divided
leaves edged with white and splashed with creamy
yellow, and has greenish white flowers.

PLANTING HELP   Easily
grown in good, moist well-
drained soil, in sun or semi-
shade. Hardy to –10°F
(–23°C), US zones 6–9.

Astrantia major
'Sunningdale
Variegated'

Phlox paniculata 'Norah Leigh'

Comfrey

***Symphytum* × *uplandicum* 'Variegatum'**
A hybrid between two species of comfrey,
naturalized over much of N Europe, where it is
often found by roadsides and in waste places. It
makes a clump to about 3ft (90cm) tall and wide,
and is good for lightening a dark corner of the
garden. In 'Variegatum' the dull green leaves are
prettily margined with cream, and the flowers,
which appear in late spring, are usually pinkish,
becoming pale lilac as they mature. 'Goldsmith' is
another variety with good leaves.

PLANTING HELP   Easy to grow in ordinary,
moist soil in light shade. The fleshy roots can be
divided and replanted in autumn or spring. Hardy
to –10°F (–23°C), US zones 6–9.

Variegated Iris

***Iris pallida* 'Variegata'**   A very attractive plant,
valuable not only for its striped, whitish yellow
leaves in autumn, but also for its wonderful pale

Symphytum × *uplandicum* 'Variegatum'

lilac-blue flowers produced freely in late spring. The spreading clumps send up branched stems to about 4ft (1.2m) tall.

PLANTING HELP   Easily grown in ordinary garden soil in a sunny position. The rhizomes can be divided and replanted after flowering or in September; if the clumps become overcrowded you will need to divide them every other year anyway. Hardy to 10°F (−12°C), US zones 8–10.

Phlox

***Phlox paniculata* 'Norah Leigh'**   There are many varieties of the garden phlox, which bring a variety of flower colours and a spicy scent to the herbaceous border in high summer, but this is one of the few with good variegated foliage. If grown well, this will make a clump to about 3ft (90cm) high, with cream variegated leaves and pale lilac flowers.

Sisyrinchium striatum 'Aunt May'

PLANTING HELP   All types of *Phlox paniculata* prefer good, fertile, moist soil in a sunny position; they do not do well on chalk or clay. Unfortunately they are prone to eel-worm, so be sure to obtain good young plants which have been propagated from root-cuttings. Hardy to −10°F (−23°C), US zones 6–9.

Variegated Sedum

***Sedum alboroseum* 'Mediovariegatum'**
There are many kinds of Sedum, most of them grown for their flowers, but this form is notable for its strange foliage. It makes a clump to about 1ft (30cm) high, and twice as wide, of succulent, grey green leaves splashed with cream. In early summer flat heads of starry white and pink flowers appear.

Iris pallida 'Variegata' at Wisley

PLANTING HELP   For well-drained, ordinary soil in full sun. Propagate by division from autumn to spring. Hardy to 0°F (−18°C), US zones 7–10.

Sisyrinchium

***Sisyrinchium striatum* 'Aunt May'**
(syn. 'Variegatum')   An upright plant, to about 1½ft (45cm), this has striped, greyish iris-like leaves and bears numerous creamy yellow flowers on slender stems during early summer.

PLANTING HELP   This is a native of the Andes, so a little frost will not trouble it. Give it a sunny place, in well-drained soil, enriched with leaf mould if you have it. The clumps can be divided and replanted in autumn or spring. Hardy to 10°F (−12°C), US zones 8–10.

Sedum alboroseum 'Mediovariegatum' at Rosemoor

Actinidia

Actinidia kolomikta A relation of the well-known Kiwi fruit, *Actinidia kolomikta* is a vigorous climber, which can grow up to 30ft (9m) tall. It is valued for its unusual leaves, which are heart-shaped, to 6in (15cm) long, pale green with pink and cream splashed tips. The tiny white fragrant flowers appear in late spring, sometimes followed by egg-shaped yellow fruits.

PLANTING HELP This does best when grown against a wall, or supported on a pergola, arch or tree. It will thrive in partial shade in deep, but well-drained soil. Hardy to −20°F (−29°C), US zones 5–9.

Actinidia kolomikta

Hebe

There are around a hundred species of these evergreen flowering shrubs from New Zealand, and many more garden hybrids. The leathery leaves are in opposing pairs, the small flowers on narrow spikes in the summer.

PLANTING HELP Most hebes, with the exception of the prostrate species, which are tougher, are not reliably hardy in cool temperate gardens, and need a sheltered, more or less frost-free place in the garden, and possibly protection with fleece or straw in the winter. They are good in mild coastal areas, being remarkably tolerant of wind and salt, and thrive in well-drained, ordinary garden soils. New plants can be produced from cuttings of non-flowering shoots taken in late summer and grown on in a cold frame.

Rhamnus alaternus 'Argenteovariegata'

Hebe × franciscana 'Variegata'

Hebe × andersonii 'Variegata'

Weigela 'Florida Variegata' in Eccleston Square, London

Hebe × *andersonii* **'Variegata'**   This makes a bush to about 6ft (1.8m) tall and wide. The leaves are green splashed with creamy yellow, and the long racemes of pale lavender flowers appear in late summer. Hardy to 0 °F (−18°C), US zones 7–10.

Hebe × *franciscana* **'Variegata'**   This form, with rounded green and cream leaves, and lilac coloured flowers in spring, makes a compact, dome-shaped shrub to about 3ft (90cm). While *H.* × *franciscana* itself and the clone 'Blue Gem' are some of the hardiest hebes, this variegated form is slightly more tender ; it is worth a place in a sunny border. Hardy to 0 °F (−18°C), US zones 7–10.

Rhamnus

***Rhamnus alaternus* 'Argenteovariegata'**
There are many different species of Rhamnus, most of which are deciduous, but this evergreen is one of the best for variegated foliage. It makes a shrub to about 16ft (4.5m) high, and has slightly twisted leaves with grey markings and a creamy white margin. The numerous tiny green flowers are borne in clusters in spring.

PLANTING HELP   Unfussy about soil, but needs protection in cooler areas, as it is slightly more tender than some of the other forms. Very useful in coastal areas and also tolerant of city pollution. Hardy to 0°F (−18°C), US zones 7–10.

Variegated Weigela

Weigela **'Florida Variegata'**   This is a variegated form of *Weigela florida*, a deciduous shrub from China and Japan. It has arching branches, but a reasonably compact habit, to about 5ft (1.5m) tall and wide. The green leaves are edged with creamy white, and the clusters of funnel-shaped, pale pink flowers appear in late spring and early summer.

PLANTING HELP   Weigelas are easy to grow in ordinary soil and are tolerant of pollution, which makes them useful in town gardens. They should be planted during the autumn or spring, in a sunny place if possible, but not allowed to dry out. The old flowering shoots can be thinned out and cut hard back immediately after flowering, but do not prune the new shoots, as these carry next year's flowers. Hardy to −10°F (−23°C), US zones 6–9.

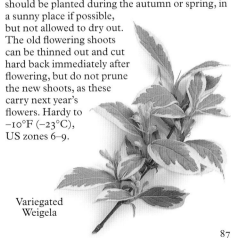

Variegated
Weigela

An ancient specimen of *Aralia elata* 'Variegata'

Aralia

***Aralia elata* 'Variegata'** A large and very handsome deciduous suckering shrub or small tree up to 33ft (10m). The leaflets are green with creamy white markings, and large clusters of tiny white flowers appear in late summer, followed by small black berries.

PLANTING HELP For acid soil, in part shade. Propagation is by grafting – not for the amateur. Hardy to −20°F (−29°C), US zones 5–9.

Dogwood

***Cornus mas* 'Variegata'** A deciduous large bushy shrub or small tree, to about 10ft (3m) tall, a native of C and SE Europe. *Cornus mas* itself has green leaves, while 'Aurea' has yellow foliage and 'Aureoelegantissima' has leaves with pink and yellow markings. 'Variegata' has green leaves edged with cream. All varieties have clusters of small yellow flowers, borne on bare twigs in early spring, sometimes followed by red oval berries. The dogwoods are a large and diverse genus of around 65 species of large shrubs or small trees, which are much used for their foliage in gardens, parks and other public places. *Cornus alba* 'Elegantissima' makes a deciduous, spreading shrub, to about 10ft (3m), high and is spectacular in autumn and winter when the

twigs become a wonderful red, contrasting magnificently, until they are blown off by winter gales, with the cream margined, grey-green leaves.

PLANTING HELP These dogwoods will do well in any reasonable, moist soil, in the sun if possible, although they will tolerate light shade. *Cornus alba* can be increased by layering and *Cornus mas* by grafting. Hardy to −20°F (−29°C), US zones 5–9.

Cornus mas
'Variegata'

Box Elder

Acer negundo   This species of maple usually makes a large deciduous tree, eventually to about 50ft (15m) or more tall, so check the amount of space in your garden before planting. If you find you have room, *Acer negundo* will give years of pleasure, as it is long-lived, and makes an attractive spreading tree with delicate and ornamental foliage. **'Flamingo'** is a form with green leaves edged with pink, which can be encouraged by trimming back the shoots in late spring. **'Variegatum'** has white variegated leaflets. On older plants, some shoots may revert to green, and these branches should be cut out if you wish to encourage the variegated leaves.

PLANTING HELP   Plant during autumn and spring, in moist, but well-drained soil in sun or partial shade. Variegated forms are increased by grafting, so buy plants from a nursery or garden centre. Hardy to −40°F (−40°C), US zones 3–10.

Variegated Elder

Sambucus nigra   This is the common elder, a native of Europe, whose flowers are used to make elderflower cordial. There are a number of forms with coloured leaves: 'Aureomarginata', with irregular yellow margins; and **'Pulverulenta'**, an extraordinary shrub which grows to about 10ft (3m) and has almost pure white leaves when young, becoming splashed with green when older.

PLANTING HELP   Elders are tough plants, and easy to grow in any reasonably good garden soil. They should be planted out during autumn or spring and can be raised from cuttings taken in autumn. To obtain better coloured foliage (at the expense of the flowers) cut the stems back nearly to ground level during mild weather in the late autumn. Hardy to −10°F (−23°C), US zones 6–9.

Acanthopanax

Eleutherococcus sieboldianus **'Variegatus'** (syn. *Acanthopanax sieboldianus* 'Variegatus') A medium-sized deciduous shrub to about 10ft (3m) high, with insignificant greenish flowers and clusters of leaflets edged with cream. This is a variegated form of the species, which is native of China and Japan.

PLANTING HELP   Although this elegant shrub is quite hardy, it benefits from a sheltered place in the garden and does best in ordinary, light soil in a warm spot. It is propagated by cuttings. Hardy to 0°F (−18°C), US zones 7–10.

White Elder *Sambucus nigra* 'Pulverulenta'

Acer negundo 'Flamingo'

Acer negundo 'Variegatum'

Variegated acanthopanax

Miscanthus sinensis 'Zebrinus'   Purple Moor Grass   *Cortaderia selloana*
'Aureolineata'

Miscanthus

Miscanthus sinensis   This group of large, clump-forming grasses grow up to 5ft (1.5m) and keep their colour right into the autumn. There are several good forms, including 'Variegatus', with creamy-striped leaves, and **'Zebrinus'**, with unusual yellow leaf-markings which become more emphatic during the summer. This last variety also produces sprays of feathery, pinkish flowers in late autumn.

PLANTING HELP   Good for ordinary, moist soil in a sunny place. All dead stems should be cut right down to the ground in about March, before the new growth starts. The roots can be divided and replanted in spring. Hardy to −10° F (−23° C), US zones 6–10.

Pampas Grass

Cortaderia selloana (syn. *Cortaderia argentea*) These well-known evergreen perennials make wonderful clumps of arching leaves and look particularly good growing near water, so that their shape is reflected. The clumps eventually reach about 8ft (2.5m) tall, with erect stems ending in silvery plumes. There are several named forms available, including **'Aureolineata'**, with gold-striped leaves, 'Pumila', which is more compact, to about 5ft (1.5m) and 'Sunningdale Silver', with very large white plumes.

PLANTING HELP   Cortaderias thrive in fertile, well-drained soil, in a sunny, sheltered site. They need plenty of room, as their eventual width will be about half the height of the plant, which is

why they are often grown as specimen plants in lawns. They need little care, although they look better if the dead leaves (be careful, they are sharp-edged) are removed in spring. They can be increased by division in spring. Hardy to 10°F (−12°C), US zones 8–10.

Purple Moor Grass

Molinia caerulea   This large, clump-forming grass is native to N Europe east to Siberia, Turkey and the Caucasus, and is naturalised in the boggy areas of North America. It is bluish green when fresh, and becomes a wonderful golden-brown in autumn. **'Variegata'** has cream-striped, arching leaves, and creamy stalks to about 4ft (1.2m) long, bearing purplish flowers in late summer.

PLANTING HELP   This is a really tough plant, thriving on acid, sandy soils, but it needs a place in full sun if possible. Hardy to −40°F (−40°C), US zones 3–8.

Ribbon Grass *Phalaris arundinacea* 'Picta' at Cedar Tree Cottage, Sussex

Striped Reed Grass

***Glyceria maxima* 'Variegata'** This grass has
clumps of strap-shaped green and cream-striped
leaves to about 2ft (60cm) tall, and sends up stems
to about 7ft (2m) high, bearing sprays of creamy
flowers in summer. It spreads by means of a
creeping rhizome, and can be invasive. A native of
Europe and parts of Asia. Hardy to –10°F
(–23°C),US zones 6–9.

PLANTING HELP   This grows naturally in
shallow water by ditches, canals and slow rivers,
indicating the ideal conditions for this plant. It
may also be grown in dryer soils, but will not make
such a fine show. Hardy to –10°F (–23°C), US
zones 6–9

Ribbon Grass

***Phalaris arundinacea* 'Picta'**   A striking
grass, making a clump up to about 5ft (1.5m), with
leaves striped with white in summer, fading to a
beige colour in winter. Spikes of cream flowers are
carried on elegant stems above the plant in
summer. The creeping roots can be invasive.

PLANTING HELP   A good plant for ordinary
garden soil, although it will also do well in damp
places akin to its natural habitat in shallow water.
Hardy to –10°F (–23°C), US zones 6–9.

Cortaderia selloana 'Aureolineata' at Wisley

Striped Reed Grass *Glyceria maxima* 'Variegata' by the water at Wilton House, Wiltshire

Chamaecyparis 'Golden Mop'

Cupressus sempervirens 'Swane's Gold'

Conifers

In recent times conifers have suffered from rather a bad press as they are frequently planted indiscriminately in unsuitable positions, and are often inappropriate in areas where conifers are not part of the natural landscape. If planted thoughtfully, however, they can provide interesting focal points, and good contrasts of shape and colour .

One point to bear in mind is that many conifers sold as 'dwarf' varieties will in time become extremely large. This may not matter, but if you are planting them on a small rock garden you may get more than you bargained for. If, on the other hand, you wish to provide a good, vertical accent in your garden, a fast-growing, upright variety will be just what you want; in other words, take especial care to choose the right plant.

Autumn leaves of Maidenhair Tree

False Cypress

Chamaecyparis This small genus is similar to the cypress (*Cupressus*), but has given rise to a much greater number of cultivars suitable for small gardens. Some of the most useful are the low-growing cultivars of *Chamaecyparis pisifera* with gold foliage, such as the slow-growing little 'Strathmore' (syn. 'Aurea Nana'), and **'Golden Mop'**, neither of which will grow to more than about 3½ft (1m).

PLANTING HELP   All *Chamaecyparis* do well in ordinary well-drained soil in sun or light shade, but the golden varieties retain their colour better if

Juniperus horizontalis 'Hughes' and *Juniperus* × *media* 'Gold Coast'

A brilliant planting of conifers at the Savill Garden, Windsor

grown in full sun. Select small plants, if possible, and plant out during autumn or spring. As with other conifers, plants can be raised from seed, but there is little point in this unless you wish to grow large numbers; coloured varieties may not come true. Hardy to −20°F (−29°C), US zones 5–9.

Creeping Junipers

There are many juniper species, and a large number of cultivars of different colour and form. The prostrate forms, such as *Juniperus horizontalis* **'Hughes'** and *Juniperus × media* **'Gold Coast'** are good for ground cover, whilst the narrowly upright forms, such as *Juniperus virginiana* 'Skyrocket' and *Juniperus scopulorum* 'Blue Arrow' are perhaps two of the best for giving good vertical accents in the garden.

PLANTING HELP   Select small plants about 2ft (60cm) high, and plant them outside in spring or autumn in ordinary, well-drained soil, in full sun or semi-shade. Hardy to −30 °F (−35°C), US zones 4–8.

Italian Cypress

Cupressus sempervirens   The Mediterranean cypress is a medium-sized tree, usually of columnar habit, and the ordinary green species, often known as the Italian cypress, is a familiar sight in Mediterranean gardens. **'Swane's Gold'**

is a more compact variety with yellowish leaves, but still makes a useful vertical accent plant.

PLANTING HELP   As for False Cypress (*Chamaecyparis*), but *Cupressus sempervirens* is less hardy and should be given shelter from cold winds. Hardy to 10°F (−12°C), US zones 8–10.

Maidenhair Tree

Gingko biloba   This deciduous tree is interesting as the last living representative of an order of plants growing in many parts of the world at the time of the dinosaurs. It will ultimately make a very large tree, to about 100ft (30m), so it is unsuitable for a really small garden, but is often slow-growing, and will usually take many years to reach any size. The notable feature of the Gingko is its unusual fan-shaped leaves, which are pale green in spring, and a beautiful pale gold in autumn. Male and female trees produce different flowers; the female are followed by unpleasant-smelling round fruits, yellow when ripe.

PLANTING HELP   Gingko will grow in ordinary garden soil, preferably enriched with some good compost, but need a warm, sunny place to thrive; they will tolerate both salt and pollution, and are good in cities. Young trees are raised from seed and should be planted in spring, or in autumn in hot climates. Hardy to −30°F (−35°C), US zones 4–10.

INDEX

INDEX

INDEX